BOOK OF RE

MW00879098

CHRISTIAN
ESCHATOLOGY

—— STUDY OF THE END TIMES ——

| • STUDY 1 • |

PRAYER M. MADUEKE

PRAYER
PUBLICATIONS
UNITED STATES

Copyright © 2021 Prayer M. Madueke

All rights reserved. No part of this work may be reproduced or transmitted in any form or by any means without written permission from the publisher unless otherwise indicated, all Scripture quotations are taken from the King James Version of the Bible, and used by permission. All emphasis within quotations is the author's additions.

ISBN: 979-8673395646

Published by **Prayer Publications**

259 Wainwright Street, Newark,

New Jersey 07112 United States.

From the Author

Prayer M. Madueke
CHRISTIAN AUTHOR

My name is Prayer Madueke. I'm a spiritual warrior in the lord's vineyard. An accomplished author, speaker and expert on spiritual warfare and deliverance. I've published well over 100 books on every area of successful Christian living. I'm an acclaimed family and relationship counselor with several of titles dealing with those critical areas in the lives of the children of God. I travel to several countries each year speaking and conducting deliverance, breaking the yokes of demonic oppression and setting captives free.

I will be delighted to partner with you also in organized crusades, ceremonies, marriages and marriage seminars, special events, church ministration and fellowship for the advancement of God's kingdom here on earth.

All my books can be found Amazon.com. Visit my website www.madueke.com for powerful devotionals and materials.

Prayer Requests or Counselling

Send me an email on prayermadu@yahoo.com if you need prayers or counsel or you have questions. Better still if you want to be friends with me.

Table of Contents

INTRODUCTION

WHAT IS DELIVERANCE?

Deliverance as a definite topic is not easily exhaustible. Most Christians do not consider the issue of personal deliverance as a duty they owe themselves. With an excellent understanding of personal deliverance, a Christian can be sure to live a victorious Christian life; not that which is void of battles of life but that with victories over life's great battles.

What Is Personal Deliverance?

- Personal deliverance involves destroying the effects of bloodline curses (see Genesis 34:25-31; 49:3-7; 2 Samuel 21:1-9).

- It is seeking to have victory over defeat one's parents suffered (see Joshua 7:1; 8:1-29).

- It is to gather your blessings or to recover scattered and stolen blessings from enemies.

Deliverance is recovering your lost or things your ancestors handed over to evil powers through sin, evil sacrifices, curses or evil covenants (see Jeremiah 16:1-4, 10-12). On the other hand, it is also important to state that deliverance is further divided into two major parts namely:

- Deliverance from sin (see John 3:16, 32, 36).

- Deliverance from the consequences of sin, physical infirmities or problems (see Matthew 10:28).

DISCOVERY OF ONESELF

Simply put, personal deliverance is a direct discovery of oneself and problems one is battling through life. This can be revealed through God's guide in times of Bible study; through vision, dream or through prayers.

God can help you discover your true self and problems through His Word. For this purpose, I advise that you go beyond reading this book ordinarily to pursuing an in-depth study of all scriptural references to see if you could discover your problems together with the right prayers to pray. This book offers you right prayers to pray to achieve desired results.

Here are important things you must do:

- You must discover besetting sinful habits, repent from them and turn wholly to God through Jesus Christ, the Savior (see Matthew 11:28-30; John 1:40-42, 45-47, Acts 8:26-37).

- You must prepare for a personal experience and relationship with Jesus Christ as your Savior and Lord.

I can write some prayers for you as a guide but if you discover the right prayers yourself, it is better than what anyone else could write down for you.

Doctors have discovered that getting patients participate in their healing process through a technique called occupational therapy have had tremendous and remarkable effects on such patients. Likewise, you must be prepared to affect your deliverance through thoughtful and deliberate actions that could help trigger your deliverance.

Before you go into the study of this book, even if you have been born-again for long, make your assurance double sure and pray this prayer:

Almighty God, I know I have broken your laws and my sins have separated me from you. I am truly sorry, and now I turn away from my past sinful habits and evils towards you. Please forgive me and help me to avoid sinning again. I invite Jesus Christ into my life to become the Lord of my life, to rule and reign in my heart forever from this day forward. Please send Your Holy Spirit to help me obey you, and to do your will for the rest of my life, in the name of Jesus, Amen.

Having prayed the above prayer, pick your writing material and write down what you hope to discover about your life through the study of this book and the areas you need prayers of deliverance as you study this book. Make a list of all your problems and your needs. There two ways to pray:

1. *you talk to God directly*

2. *You talk to your problem or the powers behind them.*

This book is divided into 34-part series to enable you study them easily. People read just to get information but when you want to get real knowledge or have understanding, experience and instruction, you need to study or learn. You need to give these 34-part series a required attention. You have to make out enough time, engage in this study and consider attentively each title in details to plot out, design and write down all you need to do in other to obtain your deliverance. If at the end you want me to be in agreement with you through prayers, you can call me or just mention my name in agreement as you pray after the program. God bless you and give you understanding as you go into this study, in the mighty name of Jesus.

CHAPTER ONE

LETTER OF INTRODUCTION FROM CHRIST

Unto Him that loved us, and washed us from our sins in His own blood"[1]

The book of Revelation, incredibly the last book of the Bible, means to unveil or uncover. It contains twenty-two precious chapters God gave to the body of Christ. Many believers view the book of Revelation as a book that is very difficult to understand. Whereas Revelation is all about the lifting up or drawing aside of a curtain, so that all can see what was unknown and hidden but now revealed and known.

When used of writing, it means to reveal or make clear (see Ephesians 3:3). When used of a person, it denotes visible presence as depicted in the following verses:

'The Revelation of Jesus Christ, which God gave unto Him, to show unto His servants things which must shortly come to pass; and He sent and signified it by His angel unto His

---

[1] *Revelation 1:5*

servant John: Who bare record of the Word of God, and of
the testimony of Jesus Christ, and of all things that he saw'
(Revelation 1:1-2).

'...So that ye were ensamples to all that believe in Macedonia
and Achaia' (Thessalonians 1:7).

One important thing to keep in mind while studying the book of Revelation is that much of its content is depicted in form of symbols. However, some of the most precious promises and prophecies in the scriptures are revealed in the book of Revelation.

The chief purpose of Revelation is to showcase Jesus, the Son of God and His future reign. God does not intend to keep the content of this book hidden from the body of Christ. Therefore, every true son and daughter of God must read and understand this book. It was previously covered but now unveiled, uncovered, revealing what was behind the veil, which was previously unseen and unknown as written here:

'Now to him that is of power to establish you according to my
gospel, and the preaching of Jesus Christ, according to the
revelation of the mystery, which was kept secret since the world
began, But now is made manifest, and by the scriptures of the
prophets, according to the commandment of the everlasting God,
made known to all nations for the obedience of faith' (Romans
16:25-26).

It is a great tragedy to be ignorant of the book of Revelation. The word *'mystery'* depicts something which was concealed or hidden, that has to be revealed before it can be understood. No one would have understood this mystery without a revelation. The truth is that it will be difficult for anyone to understand any book of the Bible thoroughly without the help and guidance of the Spirit of God. That is why believers who have God's Spirit in them are gifted to interpret and preach the Scriptures. It is a MYSTERY that has been kept out of human reach; a secret kept for ages past, but has now been revealed and must be known. This pointed is stated thus:

> *'How that by revelation He made known unto me the mystery; (as I wrote afore in few words, Whereby, when ye read, ye may understand my knowledge in the mystery of Christ) Which in other ages was not made known unto the sons of men, as it is now revealed unto His holy apostles and prophets by the Spirit' (Ephesians 3:3-5).*

Jesus Christ, the mediator between God and man was the channel through which God sent this message. The agents used in bringing the 22 chapters were God's angels and John, the servant and messenger of God.

> *'The Revelation of Jesus Christ, which God gave unto him, to shew unto His servants things which must shortly come to*

pass; and He sent and signified it by His angel unto His servant John' (Revelation 1:1).

Above verse established that God transmitted this book to Christ His son, then unto His angel, John and to the church, which involves Christians of all ages. However, it worthy to note that at the time of writing the book of Revelation, the churches were located in Asia Minor as thus stated:

'Who bare record of the word of God, and of the testimony of Jesus Christ, and of all things that he saw... John to the seven churches which are in Asia: Grace be unto you, and peace, from him which is, and which was, and which is to come; and from the seven Spirits, which are before his throne... I John, who also am your brother, and companion in tribulation, and in the kingdom and patience of Jesus Christ, was in the isle that is called Patmos, for the word of God, and for the testimony of Jesus Christ. I was in the Spirit on the Lord's day, and heard behind me a great voice, as of a trumpet, Saying, I am Alpha and Omega, the first and the last: and, What you seest, write in a book, and send it unto the seven churches which are in Asia; unto Ephesus, and unto Smyrna, and unto Pergamos, and unto Thyatira, and unto Sardis, and unto Philadelphia, and unto Laodicea. Write the things which you hast seen, and the things which

are, and the things which shall be hereafter' (Revelation 1:2,
4, 9-11, 19).

John represents God's servant, therefore this book contains messages every Christian and the entire body of Christ must study, preach or teach. This is a great privilege and weighty responsibility that must be carried out. John received this message when he was under tribulation, yet he endured and made sure it got to the seven churches in Asia. It is a huge indictment for famous preachers and ministers of our time to fail to communicate the messages of book of Revelation to our generation.

The seven churches were selected among many other churches at the time because they had in their combination all the excellences, defects, needs and duties which represent the universal church, the church of all times and land. They were selected to symbolize the whole church of God of all times. John repeatedly revealed the source of his messages, which is obviously God; the Father, Son and Holy Spirit as revealed in the following verses:

'Unto the angel of the church of Ephesus write; These things says He that holds the seven stars in His right hand, who walks in the midst of the seven golden candlesticks

⁷He that hath an ear, let him hear what the Spirit says unto the churches; To him that overcomes will I give to eat of the tree of life, which is in the midst of the paradise of God.

⁸And unto the angel of the church in Smyrna write; These things says the first and the last, which was dead, and is alive;

¹²And to the angel of the church in Pergamos write; These things says He which hath the sharp sword with two edges;

¹⁸And unto the angel of the church in Thyatira write; These things says the Son of God, who hath His eyes like unto a flame of fire, and His feet are like fine brass;

³:⁷And to the angel of the church in Philadelphia write; These things says He that is holy, He that is true, He that hath the key of David, He that opens, and no man shuts; and shuts, and no man opens' (Revelation 2:1, 7-8, 12, 18, 3:7).

Notice that Jesus introduced Himself as the first and the last, which was dead and is alive. He is the one with sharp sword with two edges; the son of God, who has His eyes like unto a flame of fire and His feet like fine brass. Jesus, the central figure of the book of revelation revealed Himself also as the One who has the seven spirits and the seven stars of God. He is holy, true with the keys of David. The door He opens, no one can shut and the door he shuts, no one can open.

Jesus is forever faithful and true, the beginning of the creation of God, I am that I am, who is without beginning, without change, without succession and without end. He is the one that revealed the book of revelation, of things which must shortly come to pass and yet many ministers of the gospel and Christians at large have abandoned or ignored this vital information to chase after miracles and unprofitable prophesies. What a tragedy! True miracle, blessing and deliverance can only come from Jesus Christ, the author and finisher of our faith; the one who owns the title deed of the earth.

THE VISIONARY

'...and of all things that he saw'[2]

Beloved Apostle John received the book of Revelation through visions he had during the great persecution of believers. The persecutors had boiled him in a drum of oil but he escaped death miraculously even though he was well advanced in age. Domitian, the Roman Emperor, incarcerated him in the isle of Patmos to suffer and die there. At that time, all the seven churches he wrote to were under persecution. Domitian employed different murderous forms to persecute the church at the time as experienced firsthand by John:

'I John, who also am your brother, and companion in tribulation, and in the kingdom and patience of Jesus Christ, was in the isle that is called Patmos, for the word of God, and for the testimony of Jesus Christ' (Revelation 1:9).

Before John saw this vision, he had written so much about Christ already. He must have thought that he has seen Christ in His fullness. On the contrary, when he saw Christ in His full glory, majesty and complete authority, he fell down at His feet as if dead.

---

[2] *Revelation 1:2*

'And when I saw Him, I fell at His feet as dead. And He laid His right hand upon me, saying unto me, Fear not; I am the first and the last: I am He that lives, and was dead; and, behold, I am alive for evermore, Amen; and have the keys of hell and of death' (Revelation 1:17-18).

Before that time, John had written all he knew about Christ in the Gospel of John. John was an apostle but in all humility that he introduced himself as a brother and companion, banished to suffer in the isle of Patmos for Christ's sake. When he saw Christ in His full authority, great beauty, glorified by God, he fell down at his feet as a dead man.

THE PERSECUTION OF THE CHURCH

"I know your works, and tribulation, and poverty..."[3]

In John's time, just like in ours today, the church was under severe persecution from internal and external forces. Throughout the ages, God has always been mindful of all the persecutions the body of Christ endures as revealed here:

Fear none of those things, which you shall suffer: behold, the devil shall cast some of you into prison, that ye may be tried; and ye shall have tribulation ten days: be you faithful unto death, and I will give thee a crown of life.

I know your works, and where you dwell, even where Satan's seat is: and you hold fast my name, and has not denied my faith, even in those days wherein Antipas was my faithful martyr, who was slain among you, where Satan dwells' (Revelation 2:10, 13).

To them that remain faithful to God until the end, God gave the following promises:

I will put upon you none other burden.

...and they shall walk with me in white: for they are worthy

---

[3] *Revelation 2:9*

I have set before thee an open door, and no man can shut it: for you hast a little strength, and hast kept my word, and hast not denied my name' (<u>Revelation 2:24</u>, <u>3:4</u>, <u>8</u>).

To them that betray God and the body of Christ, to them God also gave the following promises:

I will make them of the synagogue of Satan, which say they are Jews, and are not, but do lie; behold, I will make them to come and worship before your feet, and to know that I have loved thee.

So then because you art lukewarm, and neither cold nor hot, I will spue thee out of my mouth' (<u>Revelation 3:9</u>, <u>16</u>).

However, God is forever a faithful God. He says, *'As many as I love, I rebuke and chasten: be zealous therefore, and repent'* (<u>Revelation 3:19</u>).

It is equally important to note that at the time of Revelation, there were evil people in the congregation who made life very difficult for true believers. The profession of faith by so many of them was fake. Many Christians suffered and died at the hands of these wicked people because of their faith in Christ. Others went through trials, persecution, and incarceration and were handed over to murderous tormentors. Majority of them lived at the mercy of their enemies, where Satan's seat was, yet they kept their faith. They refused to deny Christ but remained firm to the last hours.

Antipas was maltreated by the agent of Satan in Smyrna, troubled, denied of his rights, benefits and attacked with poverty. He refused to give up his faith or blaspheme God in other to receive defiled deliverance and corrupt freedom. Antipas was bold and fearless before the wicked government of Domitian, the Roman Emperor. He chose to suffer in hunger, preferred to be cast into prison and to serve God, right before satanic throne. He died a faithful martyr, slain before his brethren, by demonic militants of the power that was.

Other faithful saints overcame evil doctrine such as the doctrine of Balaam, who allowed evil to reign and taught Barak to cast stumbling block before God's children. Wicked people at the time encouraged believers to eat things that were sacrificed unto idols and commit fornications. Only fake believers followed the doctrine of Nicolaitans that God hates.

Clement of Alexander who lived at the time that Nicolaitans practiced their deeds said that people abandoned themselves to pleasure like goats, leading a life of self-indulgence, immorality and loose-living. Liberty was replaced with license for immorality and people perverted God's grace. When this evil people from Smyrna came to Ephesus with this doctrine, the people and church at Ephesus rejected it. God commended them for standing up for sound doctrine, laboring, persevering for Christ, standing steadfast with courage and serving the Lord. Their faith was militant; a missionary faith that went after people to convert them to Christ despite all odds.

The reason for persecution was largely baseless other than hatred for truth and desire to suppress the faith that threatened the government of the day. Here are few reasons why Christians suffered great persecution at the time:

- *Preaching the gospel*: Preaching was prohibited by law and attracted severe punishments like indefinite incarceration or death. Nevertheless, fearless Christians were determined to fulfill the great commission.

- *Cannibalism*: Christians were falsely accused of cannibalism. This is because unbelievers grossly misunderstood the concept of the Lord's Supper.

- *Idols*: Christians refused to bow down to heathen idols but worshipped the only true God through His Son, Jesus Christ.

- *Loyalty*: Christians declared absolute loyalty to their Lord, Jesus Christ, the king of kings, instead of Caesar or any other principality.

- *Hatred*: Many Christians were slaves and poor, so the authorities looked down on them naturally and persecuted them easily because of cheer hatred. In those days, there was no democracy, freedom of worship or any recognized body to look into the cases of believers' complaints.

Despite what the church of Christ on earth had been through, there are still tragedies that still occur in the present day body of church. These are few present day tragedies in the body of Christ -

- It is very tragic to see believers take fellow believers to court. While some arrest or harass fellow believers with police, others kill, burn churches, fight for positions to embezzle church funds without settling issues internally, even when they have opportunities to do so.

- It is tragic to see a whole congregation fall out of love with Christ and abandon the heat and warmth of their first love. It is tragic to see a whole congregation backslide, break Christ's heart, grow cold in love for God and for one another, become orthodox and unsound in doctrine but mechanical without affection and love for God and for one another.

- It is extremely tragic for many churches of God to allow evil preachers and prophets to teach, deceive and seduce church members with their false prophecies. Any prophet, prophetess, teacher or leader that has been consumed by greed for money, immorality, pride, jealousy, anger, covetousness, and occultism or is unfaithful to his or her family must not be allowed or permitted to minister to the body of Christ no matter what.

- It is tragic to allow spiritually dead, defiled and immoral leaders to continue leading the church. We must not permit leaders who convert churches to social clubs to continue in leadership positions. There are leaders who boast of high educational qualifications, enormous wealth, etc., but in God's eyes, they are wretched, miserable, poor, blind and naked. They are spiritually dead. Their congregation is a gathering of unrepentant sinners and backsliders who profess to be Christians but are worse than sinners. They are vile, sinful, and pitiable without any robe of righteousness. They are insincere, religious, hypocritical and very hard to win to Christ than cold irreligious sinners (see Matthew 21:23-32).

OPEN DOOR FROM ALPHA AND OMEGA

*"...I have set before thee an open door"*4

The omnipotence and omniscience of God are absolute. He has all the power and He knows everything that is going on under the sun, in heaven and beneath the earth. By His power, He gave to every faithful Christian or congregation, of any age and time, open door to preach, prosper and live above the enemy's limited power on earth; a door, which no power whether on earth or in hell can shut. God said:

'I know your works: behold, I have set before thee an open door, and no man can shut it: for you have a little strength, and have kept my word, and have not denied my name' (*Revelation 3:8*).

At some point in his ministry, Paul acknowledged this mystery when he wrote, '...I will tarry at Ephesus until Pentecost. For a great door and effectual is opened unto me, and there are many adversaries' (1 Corinthians 16:8-9).

If believers can activate their faith and trust in God to use even the smallest amount of strength, opportunity or resources available to them to fight their earthly battles, no power on earth is able to stop them from achieving greatness or fulfilling the great commission that Christ Jesus

---

4 *Revelation 3:8*

gave to His church. By the way, all power is given unto Jesus who made it clear here:

'All power is given unto me in heaven and in earth. Go ye therefore, and teach all nations, baptizing them in the name of the Father, and of the Son, and of the Holy Ghost' (*Matthew 28:18-19*).

True believers who use even the smallest amount of strength, opportunity or resources available to them to fight can keep God's Word anywhere even where Satan's seat is located. If only we could use our little strength to serve God, He is more than able to humble all satanic agents, be it Pharaoh, Nebuchadnezzar or Herod to bow and worship before our God or to die. God is capable of safeguarding believers in the northeast of Nigeria, where Boko Haram[5] rages and in Southern Kaduna, and all northern parts of Nigeria where God's law is being threatened and believers are murdered continually. This is a message to the church in the northern part of Nigeria today,

'I know your works: behold, I have set before thee an open door, and no man can shut it: for you hast a little strength,

---

A terrorist group that has operated in the northern part of Nigeria for many years and are responsible for thousands of deaths of especially Christians

and hast kept my word, and hast not denied my name…Behold, I will make them (your persecutors) to come and worship before your feet, and to know that I have loved thee. Because you hast kept the word of my patience' (<u>*Revelation 3:8-10*</u>) *underlined texts in the verse are mine.*

No matter the amount of adversaries that have you besieged today, if you would only activate the power God has put on the inside of you, no matter how little, you will surely overcome the enemy. Jesus was clear about us having tribulation in this world. But the good news is that He admonished us to *'be of good cheer; I have overcome the world'* (<u>John 16:33</u>).

'You are of God, little children, and have overcome them: because greater is He that is in you, than he that is in the world' (<u>1 John 4:4</u>).

Nigeria and other countries of the world like America are blessed to have received the gift of God's Constitution (that is the scriptures) and enjoy the freedom of worshipping God among other things. Nevertheless, some wicked principalities have vowed to turn Christianity into brothels and bring the government of Satan right inside the body of Christ (see <u>Psalms 74:1-11</u>). The works of evil shall fail woefully but the counsel of the LORD shall stand strong.

Nigeria has many Christian bodies such as Christian Association of Nigeria (CAN), Pentecostal Fellowship of Nigeria (PFN), etc. Inside these bodies, there are so many Bishops, Reverends, Pastors, Preachers, Teachers, Evangelists, Prophets and all manner of professionals. The only problem with some of these bodies is that they are not using their strength in full capacity to resist the enemies of the gospel in police stations, National assemblies, the courts, etc. Their potentials have become depressing. Some of these bodies are ready to compromise their faith and sell their birthrights. They are not using their positions, abundant grace, financial provisions and huge human resources to fight the adversaries assigned by the devil to close the doors opened to us by God. Inside PFN, CAN, etc. are professional lawyers, Senior Advocates of Nigeria (SAN), professors of Law in Parliament, Executives, Ex and serving Ministers but we are not hearing them condemn in strongest terms the attacks on Nigeria churches and places of worship.

We do not hear their voices in the lower or Supreme Courts when the door opened by God is being threatened in the north, south, east and western parts of Nigeria, and even in the parliament. Do they not know that silence of Christians in the face of evil is capable of blocking access to doors that God had opened to the church, paralyze the church of God and subject them to bow to Islamic laws instead of the constitution of the land? It is wrong to keep quite when the door opened by God is under attack by the wicked principalities. It is wrong to be neither cold nor hot, no matter your reasons. God is warning all of us this day, '...*because thou art lukewarm, and neither cold nor hot, I will spue thee out of my mouth*' (Revelation 3:16).

The church has the power to confront any principality that has risen against the church and people of God. When Herod cast Peter in prison, the church, though very few, rose up in prayers. It wasn't long, the Angel of the LORD went to the prison and brought Peter out miraculously. So ought the church of our present times to do always.

> 'Peter therefore was kept in prison: but prayer was made without ceasing of the church unto God for him. And when Herod would have brought him forth, the same night Peter was sleeping between two soldiers, bound with two chains: and the keepers before the door kept the prison. And, behold, the angel of the Lord came upon him, and a light shined in the prison: and he smote Peter on the side, and raised him up, saying, Arise up quickly. And his chains fell off from his hands....' (Acts 12:5-7)

This shows that if church could use even the smallest amount of power God has given to her through His Son Jesus Christ, every oppressor will be humbled before the church, Christ's beloved.

One of the biggest problems in our churches today is that membership is no longer tied to genuine spiritual experience. There is a big difference between church attendance or bearing a Christian name and being a thoroughbred Christian. True church attendance and church membership is likened to belonging to a family and is called the body of Christ, a flock or vineyard. The state of our churches must be measured by spiritual experiences, love, faith, prayer life, knowledge and obedience to the Word of God by members. Unfortunately, many idol worshippers, occult members, wicked sinful people today claim to be Christians without the power of God working in them.

A natural man, that is man in his unregenerate state, is spiritually dead. It is therefore wrong for any nation to tolerate counting of the dead and foreigners among its citizens. Whoever is still under the control of sin, or fears losing his position because of obedience to God, or fears authorities, the princes, powers and principalities of this world more than God is a child of disobedience because he fulfills the desires of the flesh and he remains under divine wrath because he is not a follower of Christ.

Faithful Christians are those who have repented, confessed their sins, forsook them and their names are written in the book of life. Such people do all things without pride; they give credit to God for every progress and success. They work in harmony, motivate each other to live holy. They pray together and fight every enemy of their blessings. They are sanctified, filled with God's Spirit, fellowship together, love and forgive each other, keep healthy relationship with each other, recognize the place of others in the body of Christ. They speak, act, minister in co-operation, not in competition with anyone. They respect and obey the leadership of the church. Are you one of such people?

USING YOUR LITTLE STRENGTH TO SERVE

'...he had served his own generation by the will of God'[6]

Born-again experience is the best thing that could happen to any Christian while on earth. And when you are born again, God expects that you use everything you have to promote His kingdom here on earth. Believer's position, time, money, talents, gifts, energy must be used to please God. David with a wonderful combination of personal bravery, courage, boldness and skill led Israel to subdue all her enemies.

He laid the foundation of slaying giants in Israel, which a number of his officers followed suit. The major secret of his victories was that he regarded and fought Israel's enemies as God's enemies and dedicated his spoils of war unto the Lord.

'Them also king David dedicated unto the LORD, with the silver and the gold that he brought from all these nations; from Edom, and from Moab, and from the children of Ammon, and from the Philistines, and from Amalek' (1 Chronicles 18:11).

---

[6] *Acts 13:36*

In the New Testament, David was honored and remembered as one who *'served his own generation by the will of God'* (Acts 13:36).

His communion with God during his years of toils and wondering in the lonely hills manifested in the Psalms, which he composed. The care of his flocks, the perils and deliverances he obtained from God, the grief and joy of his lowly position prepared him for the work of God and defense for the truth. As a worker in God's vineyard, you must be contented with what you have believing God for His real plans for your life to manifest instead of looking for fake powers and fame that will certainly thwart your relationship with God and cut short your ministry.

As a legislator, magistrate, judge or a staff in the executive branch of the government, you must defend the truth, which is the gospel of Jesus Christ and His righteousness at all times and in all places. If you are already promoted, you must remain humble, faithful and must not allow flattery of people and pride to rob you of your place in heaven.

David had a humble spirit and was always conscious of his lowly family background, place of birth, occupation and service in the king's court. As a shepherd of his father's flock, servant to Saul and friend to Jonathan, he was very loyal and devoted. His reign was purely free from idolatry and he was loyal to God in his testimony and worship.

Through the ages, in the midst of crooked and perverse generations, God always finds people to choose and call to His service. Will God find you? You may be old now or maybe young, an ordinary member of your church, a civil servant, poor or rich, illiterate or educated. God is calling you to preach the truth of the Gospel to the world. As a student, trader, etc., you are in the mind of God, who is able to bless you beyond your imagination. Therefore, remain consistent and stay on the right path. Let us fight to keep the open door before us and avoid the mistakes of believers before us; such mistakes that caused ungodly nations to possess the inheritance of God's children. Let me share what I read somewhere:

Turkey is in the present day Europe and partly in Asia. Apostle Paul was a citizen of Turkey because Tarsus exists in Turkey. Christianity existed in Turkey for about 1,023 years while Christianity has only existed in Nigeria and Ghana for only 172 years starting from when Rev. Birch Freeman arrive at Badagry in 1842. The seven churches Jesus spoke to in Revelations 2 & 3 (Ephesus, Smyrna, Pergamum, Thyatira, Sardis, Philadelphia and Laodicea) all existed in the old Turkey. The disciples were first called Christians in Turkey (Antioch). Turkey once had the largest Christian auditorium in Europe called Hagia Sophia in Constantinople. Apostle John took Mary, the mother of Jesus, to Turkey and until date, her room has become a tourist center. However, how is Turkey today?

TURKEY TODAY

Present day Turkey now has 96% Muslims and 0.02% Christians, (less than 130,000). Muslims took over the Hagia Sophia (once largest church in Europe), converted it to a mosque for over 400 years, and later used it as an Islamic Museum. WHY, you ask? Here are things that cost Christian Turkey its honored heritage on earth:

Emphasis on doctrinal differences weakened the Turkish church.

Rivalries amongst denominations, carnality, envying, strife and divisions were prevalent. They forgot that Paul warned the church about 'I am for Paul, I am for Apollos' mindset.

Petty politics in churches coupled with ethnic biases, tribal sentiments and selective judgment or preferential treatment.

The Turks were building big cathedrals instead of building men. There was the absence of teaching ministry and lack of emphasis of new birth and discipleship.

Osman Ghazi discovered the disunity amongst Christians and used it to fight a Jihad that led to a mass genocide of the Armenians, the Hellen and Turks of that day. In fact, a Turkish Christian was the person that designed the weapon of war used in destroying the church.

Many Christian women converted to Islam to save their lives and some were raped and killed.

Osman Ghazi started the Ottoman Empire, which gave Muslims political post and made it a religion of the state. Is Nigeria and Ghana heading the way of Turkey?

Virtually, Nigerian and Ghanaian churches have made all the mistakes the church in Turkey made. We are building Cathedrals at the expense of disciplining men. There is huge disunity amongst churches. Ethnicity is the order of the day in the churches. Denominational rivalry, sharp divisions along doctrinal lines are prevalent.

More Facts

- The spiritual foundation of Turkey is stronger than that of Nigeria and Ghana, and Christianity existed for over 1000 years in Turkey unlike ours, which is only 172 years, but Islam radicalism uprooted the church in Turkey. If it can happen in Turkey, it can also happen here, if we are not careful.

- The menace of Boko Haram has destroyed many churches in the Northern Nigeria and it may take another 200 years to evangelize Borno State alone.

- There is a secret agenda to Islamize Nigeria and other African nations as contained in Abuja declaration of 1989.

- Do not say it cannot happen here. If we fail to right our wrongs as a church, then disaster is imminent. God forbid!

SOLUTIONS

- HEART-FELT Intercession for the church

- *Aggressive evangelism*: The terrorist reached out to the youths in northern part of Nigeria by giving them AK-47 and bombs. If we had reached out to them on time, they will be carrying Bibles today.

- *Support for Missions*: God is holding the church responsible for Boko Haram, yet we are blaming the government. If we had supported missions and Missionaries, we would have won those insurgents to Christ long ago.

- *Unity*: The unity of the church is key in winning this battle.

- *Political relevance*: Christians should be actively involved in politics. There must be an end to political domination by Muslims who have hidden Islamic agenda.

In the late 1990s, the Muslim world promised that by year 2020, the Mayor of London would be a Muslim. They started working very hard for it. They did not have to wait that long, they just achieved that feat, 4 year ahead of the deadline. Sadiq Khan, born in 1970, and whose Father was a bus driver that immigrated to the UK from Pakistan in the 1960's became the first Muslim Mayor of London. He is a Briton, but a Muslim. He ran for election on the platform of the Labor Party and won convincingly.

Muslims are never in a hurry to achieve their set goals. They give it time to actualize. They never relent. He defeated a Millionaire, Zac Goldsmith, who incidentally is a Jew and obviously enjoyed the support of the present Prime Minister - David Cameron. Guess where he was sworn in: Inside the Southwark Cathedral; a church.

The swearing in was done by a Reverend Gentleman. Trust that he would have sworn by a Quran only, and not a Bible. When he entered the Cathedral, guess what he did as the people gave him a standing ovation. He Announced Loudly, "I am Sadiq Khan, and I am the Mayor of London." That was significant. He was saying to the Christians "We have done it." Luke 16:8 says, 'For the Children of this world are in their generation wiser than the Children of Light.'

May the Lord help us all. Another question of great importance is, while their Islamic agenda is moving on, where and how are we executing our own Christian agenda? Have we not refused to preach the gospel of Jesus Christ? Which is the Christian agenda?

The Central Bank of Nigeria granted Jaiz Bank a national license to operate Islamic interest-free banking in all the 36 states of the Federation. The Sultan of Sokoto, who is the head of all Muslims in Nigeria, has warned that being an Islamic bank, whatever Jaiz does must conform to the rules and regulations of Islam.

Jaiz has also set up Takaful Islamic insurance. Brethren, the game plan is this: the Islamic religion wants to control the economy, but wants to do it in a subtle 'legal way'. He who controls the economic power controls all. Remember that the richest man in the whole of Africa is Aliko Dangote. He controls 54% of the nation's industries not only in Nigeria but in other parts of Africa. You do want to pray for the church now, right?

Very soon, you, your children, or siblings will be looking for jobs at Jaiz Bank or Jaiz Insurance and you will be asked as part of the conditions of service to wear hijab to work. You will be compelled to pray five times a day because they will compel all workers to pray their prayers. Do not forget that they will ask you to work on Sundays and of course, they will give you fantastic pay until they finally buy your souls over to Islam. If you are already married, they will force your kids to attend their Islamic schools because they would have attached your job incentives to it as part of the conditions of service. Soldiers of the Cross, why won't you arise in the place of prayers that God should thwart the counsels of the ungodly? Why won't you mourn like Mordecai, Esther and the Jews in a time like this?

The end is near. If the horror fails to materialize fully in our days, what about our children? O, brethren, it is time to arise and pray as never before. If your pastor has not shared this information with your church all these years, then something must be wrong somewhere.

I asked myself this strong question everyday: Can I really lay down my life for the sake of Christ and His gospel? Please take time to read this, it will definitely help.

This is a true story. During the period of the persecution, a certain woman determined that nothing would make her to recant her faith in Christ. She had opportunity to run away from her country, but she was there until the persecutors captured her; over 300 angry people with big sticks and cutlasses specially designed to administer excruciating deaths to condemned people.

However, this woman was also pregnant with twins. Her husband had already denied her publicly. One of her daughters had already been killed, yet, she was not moved.

Until that evening, when the men of the council came, it was a big show. The most painful part is that her husband led the persecutors to where his wife was. With those big sticks, they started hitting her. When they were through for the day, they tied her on the tree. She was there until the next evening.

She was crying for she was hungry. She was enduring excruciating pains. The children in her womb were hungry too but there she was, tied under ant-infested tree. Ants were biting her. There was no food or water for her so she cried until the next morning.

When the day broke, passersby were going to beat her for fun and mock her because she was accused of being bewitched. For the fact that this woman was well educated and massively respected, it took her persecutors over two hours to decide how best to kill her, so that her death would be shameful and very painful.

Only a handful few had pity on her but were afraid to identify with her for fear of death. While she shivered because of hunger and thirst, yet the smiles on her face was radiating so much that the men who were torturing her became furious. "How could someone we have tortured this way for a whole day look happier than us?" they asked themselves. They could not understand it! Finally, they brought her out and told her, "Look at this man, he is your husband. Look at that man, he is your church leader." They showed her all those that have denounced Jesus and renounced that He did not rise from the dead; that he was an impostor. "We give you the final opportunity to denounce this man Jesus, we will set you free and restore to you all your privileges, and you shall be promoted in the council and compensated handsomely for all the pains inflicted on you. But if you refuse to denounce Jesus, we shall look for more gruesome ways to kill you in other to tell the whole council that you died like a fool," they told her.

As they threatened, her face was lighted up with radiating smiles. At the moment she heard that word 'fool', she looked up and asked her Pastor and her husband, "Did you hear them? Have you forgotten that God has chosen the foolish things of this world to confound the wise? Is it not a privilege to be a fool in the hand of God than to be wise among men?"

She quickly turned to her executioners and said to them, "Officers, instead of denouncing Jesus to gain properties and privileges from the king, I rather die joyfully." She further begged them to employ the best brains in the land to think out the cruelest way to kill her. "This Jesus you want me to denounce was killed in more gruesome way than you can ever imagine. I cannot denounce a man that left eternity and came to die for me to be saved because of few properties you have promised. Make haste to end my life in whichever way you wish. For the moment my eyes are closed, a better life will begin for me, where this Jesus shall wipe out all tears from my face," she said.

"Threaten me not with death for I died this death the day I accepted that He died for me. Threaten me not because of the children in my womb. Whatsoever betides them, I leave them before God. As for me, it is better I die with them than to die and leave them behind in a world that has turned her back on her Savior," she concluded.

As they put her inside a drum with water, and lit a fire under the drum, she began to laugh. Hundreds of people gathered to witness her execution; how she was going to boil with her unborn babies. As the water got hotter and hotter, the smiles on her face got broader and brighter. The chief executioner could not take it. He commanded them to stop and bring the woman out and when they required from him the reason, he said to them that whatever this woman believed in and was ready to die such death was worth dying for. He took the woman's hand and placed them on his head, and begged the woman to pray for him.

Under the pains, the woman muttered words of prayer for him. With that anger, the next in command ordered that the man and the woman be tied on a horse. The woman was already burned halfway. Looking at her, one can see that the babies in her womb were about to burst out. Her body was gone. Her breasts were gone yet the smile on her face was broad. As they tied them on the horse, they rode the horse throughout the rough and hilly parts of the province. By the time the riders came back, they were already torn to pieces with some of the part of the bodies of the unborn babies picked from different parts of the road.

That was how that woman gallantly died. She did not compromise even in the face of unimaginable torture. But like Jesus, even at the point of death, she converted another gallant man who made a choice to live for Jesus even though it cost him his life.

Man and woman of God, we must stop telling the body of Christ the gospel of how people sowed into our television ministries and became commissioners in governments. We must stop preaching the gospel of how people sowed into our programs abroad and got unmerited promotions in their offices. That is why the hearts of many Christians today are far from God. They do not love God. They only love what God is willing to give to them.

That is why somebody has to beg them to come to church when it is raining. That is why somebody has to beg them to come to choir practice because they have not bought new clothes. Yes, that is why the women have threatened that if God did not give them their husbands by the end of the year, they would go and live with any man of their choices. Why are we blaming them? Since they joined our churches, all we have been telling them has been about miracles, riches, marriage, jobs, contracts, scholarships etc. Do they even know that there is hell fire? How many of all these sons and daughters we brag about as members can say "If I perish, I perish" for the sake of the Cross?

Sir, you and I know that some of these people following us did not come because of the love they have for God. They are here because of the miracles we promised them. We are well aware of numerous churches they have attended previously before joining our churches. We know how many other prophets in town they were patronizing before they discovered us. And we know that they will soon stop attending our churches too if we do not deliver sharp miracles to them. Do you not think it is time to tell our people the truth? If it is only in this world that we have hope, then we are of all men most miserable.

We do not really need members who cannot be able, if need be, die for Jesus. Let us not be deceived by large crowds attending our church services. People may be calling us mega churches, but when God looks down from heaven, He may be seeing the likes of abortion clinics, where spiritual destinies of men and women are being aborted on daily basis. We may have succeeded in building wonderful and very expensive churches, but of truth, inside these our church buildings may be real decaying of souls going taking place. We now entertain sinners when they come to church. The situation has gotten so bad that worldly entertainers are now given opportunities to climb holy altars to entertain people. We now sing unholy songs in the churches. That the name 'Jesus' is mentioned in a song does not make the song gospel. Let God help us.

Our general overseers must be reminded that gathering huge crowds is not really the issue after all. It is not about the quantity, but bringing quality into the quantity.

From year to year, if none of your members in your crowd has come to tell you that he is hungry to invade places to win souls for Christ, sir, heaven may have put 'caveat emptor' on your ministry.

If an Imam could teach his followers how to live and be ready to die for Mohammed, a prophet that died and could not conquer the grave, and you see these boys wielding weapons, killing and dying in defense of a randy prophet, why would none of your members, who has been sitting under you for years be able to defend the cause of the Cross, even in the face of martyrdom? Something must be wrong with the gospel you preach or the heart from where it is coming from. Greater than what hit America and even turkey is coming to hit Nigeria if the Truth did not get back to our pulpits.

I speak as a prophet: In the next five years, if there is no spiritual awakening in Nigeria, then, fifteen years from now, you will not be able to use microphone to call Jesus on any street in Nigeria. Somebody is saying it is not possible and all the big churches and big men are deceiving you now when Moslems are busy carrying out their Agendas little by little. May God help all of us. That was the case in Turkey, but today, Christianity has gone underground in Turkey. There were also great men and women of God in Indonesia. But it got to a point when some young boys and girls whose hearts God touched were crying against compromising of the word of God in their churches and the level of spiritual comatose their ministers plunged into, but that generation called them 'sadists' who were not happy that churches were being built everywhere in town. These young men and women were accused of being jealous of the exotic cars men of God were riding because they do not have any.

But today, you cannot mention the name of Jesus in public places in Indonesia. The same Indonesia where men were miraculously walking on waters. Where even government officials were calling Christians to come and help them preach to the armed robbers in their prisons. Now, where are all those big auditoriums? It all happened because that generation did not care to raise a generation after them that would be ready to defend Jesus with their lives.

Brother, the same evil wind that blew in Turkey and Indonesia is threatening our continent Africa. But as for some of us, we have made a vow that we will not be here and watch Satan wreck the legacy of our fathers. We may not know what will happen when we would have gone to be with the Lord, but we are asking God for the grace to pay commensurate price, such that our children, even the ones unborn, will not inherit big auditoriums without God inside them.

Even if we are not able to leave behind private jets and acres of lands individually, we trust God to leave behind boys and girls that would hate sin and would not be afraid to call it sin, no matter how popular it has become.

We must raise boys and girls, men and women who will open more churches. But we will also raise boys and girls who will close many more churches. They may not be perfect, but in their weakness, grace will be speaking for them and they will never compromise.

They will have money and money will not have them. We shall raise celebrities who will be signing autographs, but you will still be seeing them in malls preaching the gospel and persuading people to accept Jesus.

Sir, that generation will soon be on earth. God has not released them to us yet because He has not seen Himself in our hearts. The only thing He sees in our hearts are vain things that will not secure His glory in our lives.

Pray like this: Oh God, give me grace. I promise to raise a generation for you that will not denounce Your Holy Son Jesus, even in the face of death – Amen.

A CALL FOR CHRISTIAN INVOLVEMENT

The church of Christ on earth must come out of hiding and from the place of irrelevance to challenge unbelievers that are in seats of power. Most American Christians in Texas will understand exactly what I am talking about. I read a book by Rick Scarborough, *Enough is enough: A call for Christian involvement.* In that book, Rick narrated an inspiring story of a Christian's victory during an election.

He told the story of Steve Stockman, who ran for congress because he believed it was God's will for him to run. Steve, after seeing the downward spiral of the country he loved so much, decided to contest in 1990. Though he was a Republican, he received no support and very little encouragement from his party. He was defeated in the Republican primary.

Instead of giving up and walking away, he began to plan for the 1992 elections. He mobilized Christians to the polls. In 1992, people began to notice him when his opponent Jack Brooks began to attack him publicly. At the end of the election, Steve managed to garner forty-four percent of the votes in 1992. It was at that point that people suddenly began to believe that the mighty Jack Brooks could be defeated. Jack Brooks had occupied the seat since 1952. He was and still is the most entrenched politician in all of Texas politics and the longest tenured active congressional representative in the United States House of Representatives.

To Jack and the people of the United States, Steve was a total political novice, with no support base, no finances and no endorsements. Rick described Steve as one of the most optimistic men he ever met and a man who held a deep passion for restoring America to her Christian heritage. After Steve's loss to Jack Brooks in 1992, he persistently turned his focus to 1994 and refused to give up.

On election night in 1994, the impossible suddenly became possible. The run of forty-two consecutive years in Washington finally came to an end for the formidable Jack Brooks. Steve Stockman, a conservative Christian, running as a Republican received fifty-two percent of the vote. He won in one of the strongholds of Union-dominated democratic politics. The Christian people in this district stood with other conservatives and voted Steve Stockman into office and he was sworn in on January 4, 1995 in Washington DC.[7]

With God on our side, we shall win back our country to God. If you are a good person with the interest of this nation at heart, we shall pray for you and stand by your side until you are voted into power. God is searching for excellent leaders.

The prayers in this book are designed to encourage excellent leaders to rise up and equally discourage ungodly leaders. No matter how long and difficult the journey may be, we are sure to get there, in Jesus mighty name we pray, Amen.

---

[7]*Rick Scarborough - Enough is Enough, Liberty House Publishing (1996).*

You may not have recommendations from anyone or come from favored class, tribe or family. Just keep bearing the fruit, when the time comes, you will shine.

'But the fruit of the Spirit is love, joy, peace, longsuffering, gentleness, goodness, faith, Meekness, temperance: against such there is no law' (Galatians 5:22-23).

Do you remember the story of Joseph? Imagine what he went through even in the hands of his brothers. But what mattered in the end was that when the appointed time came, he ended up in the palace as the Prime Minister.

'Then Pharaoh sent and called Joseph, and they brought him hastily out of the dungeon: and he shaved himself, and changed his raiment, and came in unto Pharaoh' (Genesis 41:14).

'And the thing was good in the eyes of Pharaoh, and in the eyes of all his servants. And Pharaoh said unto his servants, Can we find such a one as this is, a man in whom the Spirit of God is? And Pharaoh said unto Joseph, Forasmuch as God hath shewed thee all this, there is none so discreet and wise as you art: You shalt be over my house, and according unto your word shall all my people be ruled: only in the throne will I be greater than you. And Pharaoh said unto Joseph, See, I have set thee over all the land of Egypt' (Genesis 41: 37-41).

In our days, God is still choosing and electing people for leadership positions. You may be an illiterate or a well-educated person but it does not matter before God. God can still use you the way you are to show forth His glory. Paul closed his law firm to answer to divine call. Later, he used his knowledge of law to appeal against the death verdict pronounced against him.

> 'And when it was day, certain of the Jews banded together, and bound themselves under a curse, saying that they would neither eat nor drink till they had killed Paul. And they were more than forty which had made this conspiracy. And they came to the chief priests and elders, and said, We have bound ourselves under a great curse, that we will eat nothing until we have slain Paul. Now therefore ye with the council signify to the chief captain that he bring him down unto you tomorrow, as though ye would inquire something more perfectly concerning him: and we, or ever he come near, are ready to kill him' (Acts 23:12-15).

Legal team of PFN, CAN and other Christian legal bodies must not allow any State of Assembly, the Presidency or even the National Assembly to pass any law against the freedom of worship of God. Believers must be presented with choices of where they wish to be tried; whether in a Sharia or civil court. Our legal Christian bodies or individual lawyers like Paul the Apostle can appeal any judgment until we get to the highest court in the land. We must not allow any local Sharia court, one state governor or constituted assembly to take us back to the local courts as was in Jerusalem to be judged.

'But Festus, willing to do the Jews a pleasure, answered Paul, and said, Wilt you go up to Jerusalem, and there be judged of these things before me? Then said Paul, I stand at Caesar's judgment seat, where I ought to be judged: to the Jews have I done no wrong, as you very well know. For if I be an offender, or have committed anything worthy of death, I refuse not to die: but if there be none of these things whereof these accuse me, no man may deliver me unto them. I appeal unto Caesar. Then Festus, when he had conferred with the council, answered, Hast you appealed unto Caesar? unto Caesar shall you go' (Acts 25:9-12).

God is calling on all Christians all over the world to network with one another, being brothers' keepers who use their little strength to serve God well.

God is telling us today,

'I know your works: behold, I have set before thee an open door, and no man can shut it: for you hast a little strength, and hast kept my word, and hast not denied my name' (Revelation 3:8).

This demonstrates that believers have been mandated in the Word of God to use all our strength to preach God's Word throughout the world (see Mark 16:15-20). God's Word, which is the divine constitution, has thus given us open doors, which no man can shut. But we must determine to use all our strength to serve the King of kings.

CHAPTER TWO

FIRST LETTER

(Revelation 2:1-7)

God is love. The nature of His love is absolute. As such, it is not in the nature of God to have anyone or people punished or judged without prior notice or warning against impending danger or evil.

The primary reason God sent the messages in the book of Revelation to the church is to counsel His children of the impending danger. God is calling for the attention of the church to inform her about the coming judgment. The letters to the seven churches put all the churches of all times in perspective. In all, we can relate to the messages as alert, alarm or signal for impending judgment.

'He that hath an ear, let him hear what the Spirit says unto the churches; To him that overcomes will I give to eat of the tree of life, which is in the midst of the paradise of God' *(Revelation 2:7).*

The warnings contained in the book of Revelation are intended to not only raise alarm but also encourage people to make amend with their lives. Unfortunately, many Christians have not heeded the warnings. As it was written, only those that have ears would hear. You may have physical ears to hear, but if you do not obey to do what is expected of you, the timely warnings will not profit you. Some other people may decide not to hear at all. How sad!

Before we delve into our study of the letters to the seven churches, we need some understanding of the background of the churches.

The servant of God, Apostle John, wrote the book of revelation about A.D. 95. The letters revealed what God expects of the body of Christ on earth. That is why it is of utmost importance to do an in-depth study of this book in order to understand divine expectations of your church.

THE CHURCH IN EPHESUS

'Unto the angel of the church of Ephesus write; These things saith he that holdeth the seven stars in his right hand, who walketh in the midst of the seven golden candlesticks' *(Revelation 2:1).*

The first letter was addressed to the church in Ephesus. Jesus made a powerful reference of Himself as *'He that holds the seven stars in his right hand; He that walks in the midst of seven golden candlesticks.'* Jesus Christ is the ultimate source of the entire book of Revelation. When John, the receiver of the messages, turned, he saw seven candlesticks. In the midst of the candlesticks, he saw the Son of man, the Lord Jesus Christ, clothed with a garment down to the foot and girt about the paps with golden girdle. In His right hand, He had seven stars and out of His mouth went a sharp two-edged sword. His countenance was as the sun shining in its full strength. He also saw seven angels representing each of the seven churches (see Revelation 1:12-16).

Writing to these seven churches indicates that Jesus is completely aware and is very much interested in everything that goes on in church. He laid the foundation of the church because He is the founder and the builder of His church.

Jesus Christ purchased the church with His blood and must be allowed to rule and reign in every congregation, ministry and gathering of the saints. Church founders, general overseers, pastors and leaders are not the real owners of the church or the congregation. Jesus Christ is and must be allowed to plan and execute His ultimate purpose to bring His reign of justice to the universe. And every minister, bishop, reverend, pastor, worker, etc., must co-operate with His leadership.

Church founders, general overseers, bishops, etc., are only but overseers ordained by God. The bible put it this way:

> 'Take heed therefore unto yourselves, and to all the flock, over the which the Holy Ghost has made you overseers, to feed the church of God, which he hath purchased with his own blood' (<u>Acts 20:28</u>).

Ministers must take heed not to see, convert or run the church as personal or family business. It is unscriptural and ungodly to run the church of Christ as a tribal or racial enterprise. The flocks of all congregations belong to God, not personal properties of church founders or overseers. Instead, church overseers must feed the flocks without condition or consideration for personal benefits. Jesus Christ paid in full the price of purchasing every member, so every flock belongs to Him by creation, redemption and adoption.

God gave all powers to Christ (see <u>Matthew 28:18</u>), even the power over His church and He has the final say of what happens to the church. Any minister or church leader who does not manage the church as directed by Christ is in error. Though Christ gave authority to church leaders to oversee His church, they must exercise such authority with the fear of

God as directed by Christ without carnal influences or partiality. The calling of God is true, as Christ has ordained and commissioned us through His Word to look after His church:

'*And he commanded us to preach unto the people, and to testify that it is he which was ordained of God to be the Judge of quick and dead*' (<u>Acts 10:42</u>).

'*Because he hath appointed a day, in the which he will judge the world in righteousness by that man whom he hath ordained; whereof he hath given assurance unto all men, in that he hath raised him from the dead*' (<u>Acts 17:31</u>).

Preachers must preach Christ and that is why they are ordained. God has set a day has been aside to bring everything we do as ministers, workers and members to judgment. God keeps records of all that happen under the sun since the world began. Ministers and church members who behave as if God will not hold them accountable of all their actions on earth are deceiving themselves. The way you treat church members, spend every dime and minister to members are all recorded in the book. Beloved, be careful how you live your life.

Jesus will judge all men righteously because He is a righteous judge. That is why He came, lived, preached, taught, performed miracles, healed, suffered, died and was raised on the third day. For this reason, God elevated Him so highly and gave Him a name that is above all names (see <u>Philippians 2:9</u>).

One thing is certain: '...*All men 'shall stand before the judgment seat of Christ'* (Romans 14:10).

For this purpose, God '...has put all things under His feet, and gave Him to be the head over all things to the church' (Ephesians 1:22).

The reason ministers are trained and ordained is to bring justice to the church. But they must judge themselves first. If you condemn others, judge them and yet commit the same offense, you will face greater judgment from the righteous judge. He is the head of the church and every minister and member must bear this in mind as you relate with others within and outside the church building.

Paul the Apostle believed that every Christian by '...*speaking the truth in love, may grow up into him in all things, which is the head, even Christ'* (Ephesians 4:15).

Therefore, it is the duty of every believer including church leaders to do the right thing always and to speak the truth without fear or prejudice but in love. Jesus Christ expects the members of His body to emulate His life not only within the church buildings but also from their homes.

THE CHURCH THAT RECEIVED THE LETTER

'*Unto the angel of the church of Ephesus write…' (Revelation 2:1).*

The church of Ephesus received the first letter. Paul was the founder of the local church in Ephesus. Aquila, Priscilla and Apollos were all instrumental in growing the church of Ephesus. They were deeply involved together with Paul in evangelism and discipleship of the body of Christ in Ephesus.

'*And Paul after this tarried there yet a good while, and then took his leave of the brethren, and sailed thence into Syria, and with him Priscilla and Aquila; having shorn his head in Cenchrea: for he had a vow. And he came to Ephesus, and left them there: but he himself entered into the synagogue, and reasoned with the Jews. When they desired him to tarry longer time with them, he consented not; But bade them farewell, saying, I must by all means keep this feast that cometh in Jerusalem: but I will return again unto you, if God will. And he sailed from Ephesus' (Acts 18:18-21).*

'*And a certain Jew named Apollos, born at Alexandria, an eloquent man, and mighty in the scriptures, came to Ephesus. This man was instructed in the way of the Lord;*

and being fervent in the spirit, he spake and taught diligently the things of the Lord, knowing only the baptism of John. And he began to speak boldly in the synagogue: whom when Aquila and Priscilla had heard, they took him unto them, and expounded unto him the way of God more perfectly' (Acts 18:24-26).

The Word of God grew mightily in Ephesus and prevailed over the entire city. The foremost ministers Paul trained at Ephesus to continue in the ministry were not only eloquent but also mighty in the scriptures. They were instructed in the way of Christ thoroughly. They were fervent in the spirit. They were teachers thought by Paul for three years before they were commissioned, ordained to teach others. They were diligent and taught diligently the way of the Lord.

Paul and his team preached Christ and His cross without fear of death and did not manipulate the church for material gains.

'And he went into the synagogue, and spake boldly for the space of three months, disputing and persuading the things concerning the kingdom of God' (Acts 19:8).

Healings were rampant.

'So that from his body were brought unto the sick handkerchiefs or aprons, and the diseases departed from them, and the evil spirits went out of them' (Acts 19:12).

Fear fell upon the city and Christ was magnified.

'And this was known to all the Jews and Greeks also dwelling at Ephesus; and fear fell on them all, and the name of the Lord Jesus was magnified. And many that believed came, and confessed, and shewed their deeds. Many of them also which used curious arts brought their books together, and burned them before all men: and they counted the price of them, and found it fifty thousand pieces of silver. So mightily grew the word of God and prevailed' (Acts 19:17-20).

Opposition to truth concerning Jesus Christ and the kingdom of God grew stiff.

'And the same time there arose no small stir about that way' (Acts 19:23).

'...But I will tarry at Ephesus until Pentecost. For a great door and effectual is opened unto me, and there are many adversaries' (1 Corinthians 16:7-9).

A true minister empowered by God will always speak the truth with boldness no matter the consequences. Paul preached in Ephesus for two years and all that were in Asia heard the gospel of Jesus Christ. Only a handful rejected the gospel. However, to those who believed, many signs and wonders were wrought in their lives.

When we preach the gospel with boldness and true Spirit of God, people will repent. Miracles will take place. Occultism will be destroyed and God will prevail

Before Paul left the Ephesus finally, he assembled the elders of the church and warned them sternly to take heed to themselves and the flocks, which the Holy Ghost made them overseer to feed. The church was dear to him and he knew that after his departure, many would rise with diverse teachings to tear down the church and the flock (see Acts 20:16-38). It was a wonderful thing for Paul to do.

The admonition of Paul is still very relevant today:

> 'Take heed therefore unto yourselves, and to all the flock, over the which the Holy Ghost hath made you overseers, to feed the church of God, which he hath purchased with his own blood' (Acts 20:28).

Here are key things Paul counseled the elders of the church at the time (*Ref:* Acts 20:16-38):

i. To demonstrate strong character as Paul did.

ii. Serve God with all humility of mind, with tears, temptations, troubles and persecution in and outside the church toward believers and unbelievers.

iii. How he kept nothing that was profitable for their use, lived exemplary life among them and taught them publicly from house to house with love and grace.

iv. How he ministered to the religious Jews, unbelievers, the Greeks, the wise and the unwise presenting nothing but the gospel and faith only through Christ.

v. To feed the church they are overseeing by the power of the Holy Spirit, which God has purchased through the blood of His Son.

Today, Paul's life and ministry is a model for church founders, general overseers, ministers and workers. His life, both public and private, was without blame. Every minister called by God must live a blameless life; a life of purity in order not to be a stumbling block to the flock of Christ. Paul revealed the secret of his success in ministry often.

Nothing '...move me, neither count I my life dear unto myself, so that I might finish my course with joy, and the ministry, which I have received of the Lord Jesus, to testify the gospel of the grace of God' (Acts 20:24).

For that reason, there is no need for envy, fighting, and hatred, struggling for position and killing of one another. Paul exposed those he taught to God's counsel and how to rely on God's power alone. He never allowed them the opportunity to fight each other, create quarrel, division or covet silver and gold to satisfy themselves or anyone.

Another important thing Paul demonstrated in ministry is his ability to accept and remain a godfather to Timothy because Timothy was of the same faith with him, not because he was his relation, from the favored tribe or race.

'...*Unto Timothy, my own son in the faith: Grace, mercy, and peace, from God our Father and Jesus Christ our Lord*' (1Timothy 1:2).

Today, God is warning godfathers whose spiritual sons and daughters are their tribesmen and women only. Christ is warning ministers who encourage their spiritual sons, daughters through their lifestyles to steal, commit immorality, and practice witchcraft knowing their backslidden godfathers would protect them. Spiritual sons and daughters of backslidden godfathers who commit atrocities with reckless abandon must know that the Day of Judgment is coming. Timothy, the spiritual son of Paul, received the leadership mantle to pastor the church at Ephesus and Paul instructed him to charge other leaders to teach sound doctrine.

THE CITY OF EPHESUS

Ephesus was the greatest city in Asia Minor. But the official capital of Asia was Pergamos. A Roman historian called Ephesus the light of Asia. It has the greatest harbor in Asia Minor. The city of Ephesus was very important because of its high commercial viability and that was why it was called the market place of Asia. In addition, Ephesus was the center place for big games and many people came to Ephesus from different part of Asia for games. It was also a spiritual stronghold of the devil and the center for the worship of the goddess, Diana, whose temple was built in Ephesus. The statue of Diana, the goddess, was located in Ephesus and was one of the seven wonders of the ancient world. The sale of idols was a big business in Ephesus. In Diana's temple, little gods were sold to idol worshippers.

This is the city where Paul contended with the forces of darkness, preached the gospel, had converts and raised elders and overseers. This was the city he was headed when he made the famous declaration,

'I will tarry at Ephesus until Pentecost. For a great door and effectual is opened unto me, and there are many adversaries' (Corinthians 16:7-9). The church in Ephesus was privileged to receive one of the letters to seven churches in Asia.

Paul remained in Ephesus despite attacks and persecution he encountered. Great door opened to him with many adversaries but he remained faithful to the end. This proves that it is not out of place to face adversity in your place of ministry. No matter what city, village, community or country you find yourself as a minister, get ready to contend with strongholds that control the environment. Running from place to place looking for easy life and ministry is an awkward idea. Bribing your godfathers or doing everything possible to be transferred to big church branches is not noble either.

If you are not doing the right thing, which is preaching of sound doctrine, the powers in a city may not trouble you. Financial and material prosperities without genuine salvation of your members or their names being written in the book of life cannot be called ministerial success. Every testimony without the testimony of salvation is as empty as nothing. Salvation of human souls is the pillar and foundation of Christianity. Every preaching, teaching and ministry that fails to produce true repentance of hearers is incomplete, mockery and falls short of the purpose of ministry. You can pray, preach, teach and conquer the god of mammon in any city. You can build the biggest cathedral, have the biggest congregation, and become the richest minister in the city or country. However, if the people are not genuinely repenting and turning to Christ in love; if demons are not completely dislodged in the heart, you have achieved nothing.

As a true minister of the gospel, do not be afraid of what people would say of your unadulterated preaching. Do not be concerned whether your message is adjudged unpopular and rejected. More so, do not fear whether co-ministers or your superiors would be hurt by the pureness of your message. In ministry, the only one to fear is God Himself, who rewards the works of men. And as Jesus puts it:

> 'And fear not them, which kill the body, but are not able to kill the soul: but rather fear him, which is able to destroy both soul and body in hell' (_Mathew 10:28_).

Paul's message reached to the very foundation where goddess Diana's worship stood. Paul's message scattered the bottom and the first layer of the evil throne, which was why the idol's priests prevailed upon the people to revolt. Paul's ministrations revealed the foolishness of idolatry, occultism, sin and manipulation. As a result, unbelieving gentiles and people that profited from the worship of Diana through trade revolted.

> 'And the same time there arose no small stir about that way. For a certain man named Demetrius, a silversmith, which made silver shrines for Diana, brought no small gain unto the craftsmen; Whom he called together with the workmen of like occupation, and said, Sirs, ye know that by this craft we have our wealth. Moreover, ye see and hear, that not alone at Ephesus, but almost throughout all Asia, this Paul hath persuaded and turned away much people, saying that they be no gods, which are made with hands: So that not only this our craft is in danger to be set at nought; but also that

the temple of the great goddess Diana should be despised, and her magnificence should be destroyed, whom all Asia and the world worshippeth' (Acts 19:23-27).

Paul's ministration even affected the tradition, theory and theology of the Jews. He said, *'Beware lest any man spoil you through philosophy and vain deceit, after the tradition of men, after the rudiments of the world, and not after Christ'* (Colossians 2:8). The Jews and occult grandmasters also raised alarm against Paul. You should never be afraid to take on the strongmen and altars that take cities and people hostage.

As a minister or member of the body of Christ, if witches and wizards are comfortable with your ministry or church, then something is seriously wrong with your church or ministry. For wrong reasons, if fraudsters, gamblers, prostitutes and occult members are part of your ministerial team, or worst still, among your pastors, then your ministry is not yet in touch with the light of Christ and gospel.

If wicked sinners and occult people are the ones sponsoring your ministry and handling your church's projects while true believers watch on, something is wrong. In your church, if the businesses of true children of God are dwindling while those of evil ones are prospering, your church must rise up now. If burial ceremonies, hospital cases, police and court cases outpace marriage ceremonies, child dedications, corporate business relationships, house warming, etc., your church needs to wake up from spiritual slumber. If you have so many prophets, prophetess, prayer warriors, and deliverance ministers and yet true deliverance are few, you need to start seeking for real power from Christ.

Examine your spiritual state, otherwise, you may be laboring for someone profiting from other people's foolishness. In the city of Thyatira in Macedonia, Paul encountered a young and beautiful young girl possessed with a spirit of divination, which brought her masters much gain by soothsaying (Acts 16:16). But when Paul rebuked and cast out the demon in the young girl, the hope of gains for her master was gone, the masters caught Paul and Silas, and drew them into the marketplace unto the rulers (Acts 16:19). Therefore, the idea of using other people's destiny in the form of spiritual ability for material gain is real. Many churches exist in which occult people use other people's destiny to make much gain. We refer to them as destiny quenchers, destiny killers or soul traders.

Demetrius, an occult grandmaster and other workers of like occupation in Ephesus ganged up against Paul. They were in charge of altars that controlled lives and destinies of all the unbelievers in Ephesus and the whole Asia. Every sinner or unbeliever had an occult material representing such person in evil altars. Majority of unbelievers were not aware that their lives, destinies and marriages are caged in evil altars of Diana. Also, many believers who were born again but still had old things that had not pass away in their lives, were also ignorant that their destinies, marriages, health, business, etc., were in the altars of Diana. Though they were born-again but the things that supposed to make them happy were caged, confined and arrested in the altars of Diana. They were waiting for old things to pass away without prayers of deliverance, warfare and confrontation. Many of them could have died true children of God and made heaven without experiencing God's plan of marriage, prosperity, divine health, etc., for them.

The people of Ephesus were utterly bewitched by goddess Diana. That was why when Paul and his team were accused falsely of degrading the worship of Diana in Ephesus and persuading people to turn away from idol worship, thereby putting idol craftsmen's jobs in danger, the whole city erupted.

'And when they heard these sayings, they were full of wrath, and cried out, saying, Great is Diana of the Ephesians. And the whole city was filled with confusion: and having caught Gaius and Aristarchus, men of Macedonia, Paul's companions in travel, they rushed with one accord into the theatre. And when Paul would have entered in unto the people, the disciples suffered him not. And certain of the chief of Asia, which were his friends, sent unto him, desiring him that he would not adventure himself into the theatre. Some therefore cried one thing, and some another: for the assembly was confused; and the more part knew not wherefore they were come together. And they drew Alexander out of the multitude, the Jews putting him forward. And Alexander beckoned with the hand, and would have made his defence unto the people. But when they knew that he was a Jew, all with one voice about the space of two hours cried out, Great is Diana of the Ephesians' (Acts 19:28-34).

'And I saw the woman drunken with the blood of the saints, and with the blood of the martyrs of Jesus: and when I saw her, I wondered with great admiration' (Revelation 17:6).

'Therefore, if any man be in Christ, he is a new creature: old things are passed away; behold, all things are become new' (2 Corinthians 5:17).

It is a very sad thing for a Christian, who lives a holy and sanctified life, to sit by and wait for old things to pass away and they never did. While some Christians live their lives complaining, others backslide and die without experiencing the joy of being married, financial miracles, healing and true deliverance from all their problems. Others manage to hold on to the faith but never saw wicked old things such as ancestral bondage, generation barriers and limitations pass away. Many die as Christian martyrs and go to heaven, but the truth is that while on earth, they never enjoyed victorious living. The reason is that the principalities in-changer of their problems sat permanently on their blessings, destinies and all that God assigned to them on earth.

We cannot separated such people from the group of people mentioned in <u>Revelation 17:15</u>, *'...The waters which thou saw, where the whore sat, are peoples, and multitudes, and nations, and tongues.'*

Though the Christian life is a life of victory, it is also a life of warfare. Paul states in <u>2 Corinthians 10:3-5</u>, *'For though we walk in the flesh, we do not war after the flesh: For the weapons of our warfare are not carnal, but mighty through God to the pulling down of strong holds; Casting down imaginations, and every high thing that exalts itself against the knowledge of God, and bringing into captivity every thought to the obedience of Christ.'*

Many Christians while quoting 2 Corinthians 5:17, *'Therefore if any man be in Christ, he is a new creature: old things are passed away; behold, all things are become new,'* fail to resist the old things in their lives after being born-again. Sometimes, those that resist do not resist enough. They just keep asking without seeking or knocking. Perhaps, they do not understand how to engage in spiritual warfare. It behooves on every Christian to know how to put on the whole armor of God, pray all manner of prayers, cast down imaginations and bring the powers in-charge of poverty, sickness, etc., to obey Christ's plans and promises concerning their lives.

When Paul arrived in Ephesus, the first thing he did was to downgrade the power of Diana. In like manner, God expects every believer's life to be hot not cold. If Paul's life was cold, do you assume he would have achieved what he achieved in Ephesus? You need to confront the powers in-charge of your family's blessings, wealth and all good things your ancestors lost in order to recover all your family's blessings and wealth. When Paul's prayers dismantled the powers of goddess Diana, Demetrius and other highly placed individuals rose up, loosed all the city boys, men and women in their altars and they trooped to the streets of the city to riot against Paul and his teachings.

There are always a few wicked but powerful people, who control every city. They can speak to their altars and their captives would begin to misbehave. If they want human sacrifice, they would consult their evil altars in their houses to control people through witchcraft to commit murder or suicide.

Child of God, this is eye opening. Some strange occurrences in so many peoples' lives are products of manipulation. Against your will and reasoning, anytime you beat your wife, commit adultery, fall sick, disagree with people, lack anything, etc., it could be someone is in some altar doing some enchantments against you. If you are a drunkard, smoker, husband snatcher, rapist, etc., it could be that someone is manipulating your destiny in some evil altar. Anytime you become sick, have pains, miscarry or fail to conceive as a married woman, you could be under the control of an evil altar. Demetrius and his group cried to their altars and the whole city was filled with confusion, problems and destructions.

'And when they heard these sayings, they were full of wrath, and cried out, saying, Great is Diana of the Ephesians.

'And the whole city was filled with confusion: and having caught Gaius and Aristarchus, men of Macedonia, Paul's companions in travel, they rushed with one accord into the theatre.

'Some therefore cried one thing, and some another: for the assembly was confused; and the more part knew not wherefore they were come together.

'And they drew Alexander out of the multitude, the Jews putting him forward. And Alexander beckoned with the hand, and would have made his defence unto the people.

'But when they knew that he was a Jew, all with one voice about the space of two hours cried out, Great is Diana of the Ephesians' (Acts 19:28-29, 32, 34).

Imagine what it was like for an assembly to gather but remain confused at the same time and cannot explain why they gathered. For more than two hours, matured men and women, even educated ones among them, cried with one voice. An arrow of confusion was released from the altars of Diana of Ephesus. The city was under this condition when Paul started a church, lived there for three years and handed leadership mantle to Timothy. The letter to this church was the first among the letters Jesus sent to the seven churches in Asia. This is the letter you and I are privileged to be reading now.

Jesus Christ praised the church at Ephesus for having remained faithful in the midst of spiritual blitz from goddess Diana and her innumerous demonic agents (see Revelation 2:2-3, 6).

Jesus began by saying, *'I know thy works...'* That means that nothing you do as a minister, worker or church member can be hidden from God. He knows your contribution in your local church, city and your home. He knows your efforts to populate or depopulate God's kingdom. Jesus commended and praised the church in Ephesus because they stood their ground for sound doctrine, laboring and persevering for the sake of Christ. They were patient and uncompromising against every form of evil. They were praised for their victory over tempters and temptress who masqueraded as apostles but are nothing but liars. Believers and leaders in the church at Ephesus were no nonsense people and did not joke with their ministry. Even though they needed more members, but they rejected ministers who proved to be agents of the devil. They were not in a hurry to ordain people as leaders, no matter how rich, influential or useful such people were.

They labored for Christ's sake only and did not allow unrepentant pastors and ministers to destroy the flocks, which the Holy Ghost committed unto their care. Ministers that were possessed by strange or immoral spirits, spirit of mammon, etc., were not allowed to take over the pulpit, no matter their academic qualification or tribe. They hated doctrines that promoted sinful lifestyles and everything that God hates. They truly proved they were the fruits of Paul's labor. Paul had beseeched them saying,

'For I have not shunned to declare unto you all the counsel of God. Take heed therefore unto yourselves, and to all the flock, over the Holy Ghost hath made you overseers, to feed the church of God, which he hath purchased with his own blood. For I know this, that after my departing shall grievous wolves enter in among you, not sparing the flock. Also of your own selves shall men arise, speaking perverse things, to draw away disciples after them. Therefore, watch, and remember, that by the space of three years I ceased not to warn every one night and day with tears. And now, brethren, I *commend you to God, and to the word of his grace, which is able to build you up, and to give you an inheritance among all them which are sanctified' (Acts 20:27-32).*

Christ praised the leaders of Ephesus church for declaring the whole truth and the counsel of God. They hated the deeds of Nicolaitans. Clement of Alexandria who lived at the time the Nicolaitans practiced their deeds once wrote, *"They abandoned themselves to pleasure like goats, leading a life of self-indulgence, immorality and loose living".* Liberty was replaced with license to sin and perversion of the grace of God. Some churches had accepted the same lifestyle and teachings of the Nicolaitans but not the church at Ephesus. The leaders and believers at Ephesus rejected the Nicolaitans and hated their deeds. But today, many pastors are willing to allow any minister to mount their pulpit with fake prophecies, signs and wonders to deceive the mind of the simple. How sad!

The testimony of Paul and his fellow laborers for all the churches including Ephesus is this: '...*We give thanks to God always for you all, making mention of you in our prayers; Remembering without ceasing your work of faith, and labor of love, and patience of hope in our Lord Jesus Christ, in the sight of God and our Father'* (1 Thessalonians 1:2-3).

However, Paul admonition is still relevant to our churches today, whereby he wrote:

'...I beseech you, brethren, mark them which cause divisions and offences contrary to the doctrine which ye have learned; and avoid them' Romans 16:17.

'For ye have need of patience, that, after ye have done the will of God, ye might receive the promise' (Hebrews 10:36).

The believers in Ephesus heeded to Paul's advice. They remained faithful to God even under severe conditions, laboring in patience and hope because they believed in God. They avoided anything and anyone that could have brought their relationship with Christ into doubts and freed their pulpits from sinful ministers.

It will not be very easy to find such church in the world today for many ministers and believers are falling out of faith in Christ and righteousness of God continually. Many have gone out of God's way to acquire power, riches, marriage, children and material things. Their hands, hearts and ways are defiled, polluted and contaminated. This ought not to be so.

Many churches and church leaders today are not patient to wait for God's time but have gone out of their ways to get more members, money and power at all cost. Even though they are still ministering, preaching and helping people, they are no longer righteous. Their names are no longer in the book of life. They have deserted the way and received defiled gifts and talents that have polluted their hands in their search for temporary strength and contaminated power.

As a true minister of the gospel, do not let your eyes deceive you and do not let your heart be carried away. Do not be deceived by gigantic church buildings, big crowds, precious things like gold and diamond, big cars, big apartments, traveling all over the world with family members and enjoying the best things of life. Some churches that are enjoying these good things of life today have soiled their ministries and all manner of abominations on earth have permeated their ministries. Enjoying good things of life is not evil. However, many ministers and members have gone out of their ways to defile their hands to get them. On the contrary, believers in Ephesus were patient and waited until their blessings came without going out of their way to acquire them. They labored, rejected evil ways and hated the deeds of Nicolaitans. The body of Christ ought to be on your guard about what is written about the great whore:

'And the woman was arrayed in purple and scarlet color, and decked with gold and precious stones and pearls, having a golden cup in her hand full of abominations and filthiness of her fornication: And upon her forehead was a name written, MYSTERY, BABYLON THE GREAT, THE MOTHER OF HARLOTS AND ABOMINATIONS OF THE EARTH' (Revelation 17:4-5).

Many pastors are corrupted because they do not want to suffer or be tenants for a long period. They do not wish to stay hungry or trek with the legs while doing ministry. They want to build the biggest cathedral in the city and know everyone that matters in government. They want to build houses and destroy members' lives with their occultism and host the biggest programs that would attract all the rich people in the city.

Paul and his fellow workers saw the work of ministry differently. Hear him:

'Therefore seeing we have this ministry, as we have received mercy, we faint not... For which cause we faint not; but though our outward man perish, yet the inward man is renewed day by day. For our light affliction, which is but for a moment, worketh for us a far more exceeding and eternal weight of glory; While we look not at the things which are seen, but at the things which are not seen: for the things which are seen are temporal; but the things which are not seen are eternal' (2 Corinthians 4:1, 16-18).

'Wherefore I desire that ye faint not at my tribulations for you, which is your glory' (Ephesians 3:13).

It was obvious that in Ephesus, God called ministers of the gospel into ministry, ordain them divinely, and empower them from heaven. That is the reason ministries in the apostolic era have heavenly mark, support and grace to succeed in God's timing. However, today, wealthy and influential friends and family members call many ministers into ministries. Some ministers are in the church for the purpose of entertainment. Sponsors with defiled and ill-gotten wealth from fraud and armed robberies call other ministers into ministries too.

This is exactly what the church of Christ is suffering on earth today. It is not easy for ministers that are called through dubious means to be patient or ready to suffer for the sake of Christ for the real power to do ministry. The fall of such ministers is usually calamitous, sudden and unannounced. While their outward appearance looks flesh, glorious, their strength expires without notice. They can die or perish without remedy under light affliction. Ministers who are not patient to wait for God's time pursue temporary things and exchange their souls and souls of their followers for earthly things.

True believers, ministers and members who are patient like the Ephesians may suffer or faint, but at the end, God will renew their lives. Any suffering, delay or denial you are going through now because of Christ is temporary. You may have a delayed promotion, ministry or remain a tenant without a car or anything to show as a true child of God but if you could really wait, and pray in hope and faith, your blessing will be eternal. The Ephesians maintained sound doctrine, laboring and persevering for the sake of Christ. They were steadfast in endurance and courageous in service to God and humanity. They hated evil practices that were common in their day that were allowed by other churches. At the end, they received a letter of commendation from Christ. If Christ writes to you now, will He praise you the way and manner you counsel your members and relate with your immediate family?

If Christ should return today or writes you a letter, are you worthy of His praise? Do you imagine that He will commend the way you handle offering, finances, seed faith, prophets offering and all the monies that come into the church? If Christ should write to you now, will he commend you the way you pursue, acquire and use things and the way you live your life?

In Ephesus, it was assumed that people who purchased little Diana goddess are powerful. Likewise, today in our churches, we fall easily for people who prophesy, gather big crowds, build big cathedrals and rate them as most powerful. We revere people who drive big cars and live in mansions without considering their spiritual worth.

In our churches today, we regard ministers to be powerful based on the amount of crowd they gather and amount of money they have, etc. It was like that too at Ephesus where people were doing unimaginable things for the sake of getting power, even from the devil. But Paul wrote to Ephesians Christians and directed them to where real, lasting and eternal power is. He wrote:

'Finally, my brethren, be strong in the Lord, and in the power of his might' (Ephesians 6:10).

Child of God, would you believe that there are general overseers, bishops, pastors, reverends, workers and ministers who are witches and wizards. They are occultist, wicked, murderers, destiny killers, fraudsters and very powerful in enchantment, bewitchment and divination. They destroy their members and sit upon their destinies. But in Paul's letter to the church in Ephesus, he informed them of the power that is in the Lord. If you want to be strong, be patient like the church in Ephesus and ask for the power that comes from the Lord. Every other power will fail but not the power of His might.

> '*And I will wait upon the LORD, that hides His face from the house of Jacob, and I will look for Him*' (<u>Isaiah 8:17</u>).

Godliness and contentment is a great gain and the ability to wait for God's power until it comes is the victory of all victories. I am a living beneficiary of God's Word as written in Job 17:9 and Isaiah 8:17.

THE CONVICTION

Despite all the good works, labors of love, great patience, endurance, courage and righteous living the church in Ephesus was known for, the all-seeing eye of God still revealed where they were failing. Christ had to point it out in this way:

'...I have somewhat against thee, because thou hast left thy first love' (Revelation 2:4).

The body of Christ in Ephesus abided in Christ but not perfectly. As the Bridegroom of Christ Jesus, they were supposed to remain pure, but at some point, they abandoned the heat and warmth of their first love. They became mechanical without affection and love. Perhaps, they had ministers and leaders who enticed them or exalted some doctrines above the Word of God. Instead of remaining steadfast in prayer and sound doctrine, they could have focused more on other things like mode of dressing, tithing, seed sowing, prosperity, deliverance, dancing, etc., and abandoned the weightier matters of the Word. Jesus had to rebuke the Pharisees and Scribes for the same offense.

'Woe unto you, scribes and Pharisees, hypocrites! For ye pay tithe of mint, anise, and cummin, and have omitted the weightier matters of the law, judgment, mercy, and faith:

these ought ye to have done, and not to leave the other undone' (Mathew 23:23).

For that reason, when you uphold one way of life far above core Christian life and values, you may eventually end up practicing witchcraft without knowing it. It is better to embrace the fruits of the Spirit above other things. The fruit of the Spirit is love, joy, peace, longsuffering, gentleness, goodness, faith, Meekness, temperance: against such there is no law (Galatians 5:22-23).

Obviously, the Christians in Ephesus prophesied, manifested God's gift, sang very well, and preached well and eloquently defended their faith. Yet, if you could relate with some of them closely, you would have seen the presence of greed, pride, immorality, finance mismanagement, jealousy, covetousness, anger and unfaithfulness in families. With fervency in their evangelism, deliverances, exploits, victory over goddess Diana and demolition of evil forces, the church in Ephesus still lacked genuine love for Christ. That was tragic because no matter the number of demons you cast out or testimonies of prosperity you share, you are absolutely nothing without love. No matter your achievements, exploits, crowd, boldness and kingdoms you have conquered, if you lack true love, you are under condemnation. Lord Jesus told the church in Ephesus that He has something against them. Your members, family and those who sing your praise may not tell you the truth but Christ will. Without true love for Christ, you break His heart. You may be the best deliverance minister that even terrifies the devil, but if you do not have love, you amount to nothing before God. You may be generous, good and gifted but if you are tribal, practice selective judgment, favor your tribe's people, give only them big branches and hate others, you fall out of God's love.

Here are some verses that speak strongly about love and how God feels about it -

'Go and cry in the ears of Jerusalem, saying, Thus says the LORD; I remember thee, the kindness of thy youth, the love of thine espousals, when thou wentest after me in the wilderness, in a land that was not sown' (*Jeremiah 2:2*).

'And because iniquity shall abound, the love of many shall wax cold' (*Mathew 24:12*).

'Having damnation, because they have cast off their first faith' (*1Timothy 5:12*).

Pure love does not discriminate or practice partiality in God's kingdom. When the Ephesians received Christ through the ministry of Paul, their love was pure, undefiled without discrimination or partial. However, by the time they received this letter, it has gone down, polluted and unfit for eternity. The forces and bombardment of iniquity has affected their love for Christ.

Pressures of life and love of things of this world can make a onetime super Christian to cast off his first love. By the time the church in Ephesus received the letter from Christ, their love for Him was weak. Remember these Christians pulled goddess Diana down. They had true and ordained ministers who challenged the evil, destroyed aggressive altars, dealt with unrepentant witches and wizards and frustrated demons on suicide missions.

Christians at Ephesus were part of few churches in Asia that blocked Nicolaitans, rejected their wayward and immoral lifestyle. They fought against coming to church naked or dressing like Jezebel. They conducted deliverances and cast out violent demons yet they fell out of love with their Savior and Lord, Jesus Christ. They became greedy, covetous, immoral and robbed God.

Jesus values every other thing you do for Him and others but your love for Him must not diminish. One of the evidences of true love for Christ is feeding His sheep. Thrice, Jesus said to Peter, '*Do you love me? Feed my sheep*' (see John 21:15-17). The primary duty of a shepherd is to feed the sheep. It is very unfortunate that many people in the ministry today are not feeding the sheep and the reason is because they have no love for Christ. They are in ministry to feed themselves, their families and friends. It is written,

> '*We love Him, because He first loved us. If a man says, I love God, and hateth his brother, he is a liar: for he that loveth not his brother whom he hath seen, how can he love God whom he hath not seen? And this commandment have we from Him, That he who loveth God love his brother also*' (*1John 4:19-21*).

Some ministers feed Christ's sheep outside the will of God and purpose. That cannot be counted as obedience to Christ. For instance, Simon Peter led the sheep, the people he converted to Christ. He loved Christ, answered God's call, oversaw the sheep Christ left behind but he had no idea of what kind of food to feed them. His major concern was to feed the sheep with physical food. That was why he went back to his occupation immediately after Jesus died.

'Simon Peter said unto them, I go a fishing. They say unto him, We also go with thee. They went forth, and entered into a ship immediately; and that night they caught nothing' (John 21:3).

Many general overseers, church founders, bishops, etc., are feeding Christ's sheep outside the will and purpose of God. They feed the sheep with physical food of false doctrines, loose living, envy, jealousy, division and all manner of lies in other to keep them in their fellowship. Out of envy, they abandon their calling and preach against other ministers. They influence their members to hate and fight fellow believers. That is not the love of Christ. Carnally minded ministers preach against deliverance, sanctification, warfare, mode of dressing, etc., yet they cannot solve problems plaguing the body of Christ. Their members toil all night and day and through life without tangible progress.

'There were together Simon Peter, and Thomas called Didymus, and Nathanael of Cana in Galilee, and the sons of Zebedee, and two other of his disciples. Simon Peter saith unto them, I go a fishing. They say unto him, We also go with thee. They went forth, and entered into a ship immediately; and that night they caught nothing' (John 21:2-3).

If your church fails to make real spiritual exploits, handle effectively challenges church members face and produce successful members with Christian characters, then you may need to examine whether your love for Christ is genuine. And if your so-called ministry lures members to sin or causes your pastors to commit immorality, become God's enemies by breaking His commandments and harm their relationship with God and others, your love is defiled.

A general overseer of a church where pastors, ministers and members hate, fight and kill each other, misappropriate church funds, practice witchcraft, patronize demonized godfathers is not feeding the lamb of Christ. A great deliverance ministry with great testimonies but without truly converted leaders and members is not a right place to feed the lambs of Christ. You may have one million branches and uncountable millionaire members but if they are not born-again, you are not feeding Christ's lambs. In your ministry, if your efforts are not labors of love, then they do not worth anything. It is written:

'Though I speak with the tongues of men and of angels, and have not charity, I am become as sounding brass, or a tinkling cymbal.

And though I have the gift of prophecy, and understand all
mysteries, and all knowledge; and though I have all faith, so that
I could remove mountains, and have not charity, I am nothing.
And though I bestow all my goods to feed the poor, and though I
give my body to be burned, and have not charity, it profiteth me
nothing' (1 Corinthians 13:1-3).

Some leaders are into deliverance ministry, while others are in prosperity ministry. There are yet others in holiness ministry. However, whatever your ministry espouses, if it cannot penetrate the human soul to bring conversion and prepare members for heaven, you may be feeding lambs that are not Christ's. Jesus convicted the church at Ephesus because though they conquered demons and overcame poverty and evil powers that kept good things from them, they abandoned their first love.

You may speak eloquently, operate with nine gifts of the spirit, learn how to preach, teach and present the truth of God convincingly, but if you do not have love, you are yet to start your ministry and journey with Christ. If you have love in your heart, opposition, gossipers or enemies cannot push you against God. If you have God's love, your reaction, manner of approach when provoked, angered, hated or crushed will not push you to sin against God. True love destroys envy, jealousy, pride, self-exaltation, self-praise, bragging or boasting. True love does not give room for rudeness. It is not ill-mannered or disorderly. True love considers others first. It seeks for the happiness of others and not self-centered. That was what Christ discovered in the lives of the Christians at Ephesus and condemned it. If you are the type that pursues things by all means necessary and at all cost, you may get whatever you are pursuing but God's love will not and can never rest upon it. But if you must pursue anything at all cost, then '...*covet earnestly the best gifts: and yet shew I unto you a more excellent way*' (1 Corinthians 12:31).

You cannot give the greatest the position of the greater. Christ is the love that God gave to us and He must be recognized and given the right place in our lives. God commanded us to love the Lord with all our minds, hearts and strength, and we must obey.

GOD'S CHARGE AND COUNSEL

One good thing about our God is His counsel, which will always stand. Jesus counseled the church at Ephesus to

'Remember therefore from whence thou art fallen, and repent, and do the first works; or else I will come unto thee quickly, and will remove thy candlestick out of his place, except thou repent' (Revelation 2:5).

That was simple obligation or requirement they must meet to compliment or balance the good things they were doing already. It was an instruction they must obey to add to what they were doing already. It was an order issued or commanded by the commander of all commanders. This is good for our learning.

This instruction was meant to be received by the church without addition or subtraction. But today, many ministers are modifying the gospel to suit their purposes and sound pleasing to their members. For this reason, God has removed the candlesticks of many ministries without them knowing. This can be likened to what happened to Samson after the Spirit of the LORD had departed from him.

'And she said, The Philistines be upon thee, Samson. And he awoke out of his sleep, and said, I will go out as at other times

before, and shake myself. And he wist not that the LORD was departed from him' ([Judges 16:20](#)).

When genuine repentance is no longer being exhibited in any church, such church is dead and cold before God no matter the amount of noise they make. A ministry without true and sincere testimony of repentance of sinners is worthless before God. Christ told the Ephesians to remember where they were and repent of their lack of love, first work. Many churches are filled with florescence or shinning bulbs when in actual sense darkness has taken over them. The Word of God is very explicit. If we continuously refuse to listen to God, then we can be sure that He will not listen to us in the time of our calamity.

'Turn you at my reproof: behold, I will pour out My Spirit unto you, I will make known my words unto you. Because I have called, and ye refused; I have stretched out my hand, and no man regarded; But ye have set at nought all my counsel, and would none of my reproof: I also will laugh at your calamity; I will mock when your fear cometh; When your fear cometh as desolation, and your destruction cometh as a whirlwind; when distress and anguish cometh upon you' ([Proverbs 1:23-27](#)).

God's promise to every believer who obeys this command is restoration, spiritual awakening, understanding and renewal of relationship. The ultimate purpose for warning us is to bring us back into fellowship with Him to release His blessings for our obedience. For those who wish to ignore this command, charge and order, they can be sure God will not help them in time of need.

God is omnipotent and omnipresent but will not manifest in the absence of your obedience. Instead, he will laugh at your calamity, mock you in times of your destruction, desolation, distress and anguish. Many people have become discouraged, confused, disillusioned and disappointed that in the midst of surplus prayers and deliverance ministries yet things are not getting better. With all these overwhelming Christian activities in the country, yet prayers are not answered. The reason is because the commands, charge and issued order from the commander-in-chief of all the commanders has been set at naught. That is why you pray many prayers, do much fasting, deliverance upon deliverance, sow seeds, pay tithes, sponsor programs, do all manner of things, yet your prayers are not answered. Did God not warn us?

'Then shall they call upon me, but I will not answer; they shall seek me early, but they shall not find me: For that they hated knowledge, and did not choose the fear of the LORD: They would none of my counsel: they despised all my reproof. Therefore, shall they eat of the fruit of their own way, and be filled with their own devices. For the turning away of the simple shall slay them, and the prosperity of fools shall destroy them. But whoso hearkeneth unto me shall dwell

safely, and shall be quiet from fear of evil' (Proverbs 1:28-33).

Many deliverance ministers ordained to deliver others are not obeying God's command. Many deliverance candidates seeking for deliverance are not obeying God's command. Many prophets, prophetess, intercessors and church leaders are not obeying God's command. That is why people call upon God in their calamity, fear, desolation, destruction, distress, suffering and the answers refuse to come. They hear God's counsel every now and then but they would not heed God's counsel. Instead, they prefer all night prayers and continuous deliverance programs.

It is foolishness to disobey God's command, set His counsel at naught, ignore all His report, despise His knowledge, refuse to be afraid of His Word and then turn around to pray for forty nights or live in the church seeking for His deliverance. If you have chosen to do things your own way, why worry God or force Him to deliver you when you are filled with your own devices? If you chose the prosperity of a fool, you must be ready to reap the destruction that is attached to it. If you want deliverance and answers to your prayers, then obey God's command, His charge and orders. The maker of heaven and earth is saying to you today -

'Come now, and let us reason together, saith the LORD: though your sins be as scarlet, they shall be as white as snow; though they be red like crimson, they shall be as wool...For

My thoughts are not your thoughts, neither are your ways
My ways, saith the LORD'(Isaiah 1:18, 55:8).

I have studied the bible repeatedly but I am yet to see anyone that was punished, suffered to death or sent to hell because he committed sin. No, not even one. People suffer to death and go to hell because they refuse to come to God through repentance and forsaking of sins. The primary purpose of God's commandment is to return us back to God in repentance. No matter how sinful, wicked and bad you are, or have been, you can still return to God and obey His commandments.

But if you chose to remain in your sinful ways, then you cannot expect God to dishonor His Word and come to your help, no matter how much you pray or how much pastors pray for you. Do not be deceived. God is saying to us every passing day -

'If my people, which are called by my name, shall humble themselves, and pray, and seek my face, and turn from their wicked ways; then will I hear from heaven, and will forgive their sin, and will heal their land' (2 Chronicles 7:14).

This is an open invitation to fellowship with God our Father, enjoying His love, blessing, guidance and protection.

'The LORD is nigh unto them that are of a broken heart; and saveth such as be of a contrite spirit' (Psalm 34:18).

No matter how big your problems are, God knows that. That is why He made provisions in advance for all solutions. The solution mostly lies in our humility to follow God's counsel; keep His command, seeking His face at all times and turning away from our wickedness.

You may argue that God has delivered people in your deliverance ministry without precondition of obedience to His commandments. That may sound true because God can even heal sinners or deliver the wicked in order to give them chance to repent. Some ministers have gone into covenant with the devil in their quest to solve problems. But the truth is that they are succeeding in postponing, transferring or suspending such problems. They do not cast out demons really. They only have demonic anointing of transferring problems from the head to the leg.

Outside of God's wisdom, you can never be wiser than Satan can. I am very sorry to reveal that many deliverance ministers and their ministries are in covenant with Satan. They are experts in these three strategies - Suspension, sent on transfer and sanction for a season. They have no divine power to cast out demons. They are swindlers, carnal and counterfeit ministers with deceptive signs and wonders, which they use to confuse the mind of the simple. Paul the Apostle wrote about them this way:

'For such are false apostles, deceitful workers, transforming themselves into the apostles of Christ. And no marvel; for Satan himself is transformed into an angel of light. Therefore it is no great thing if his ministers also be transformed as the ministers of righteousness; whose end shall be according to their works' (2 Corinthians 11:13-15).

If you desire real deliverance, then obey God's command and counsel.

He that hath an ear, let him hear what the Spirit saith unto the churches; To him that overcometh will I give to eat of the tree of life, which is in the midst of the paradise of God.

He that hath an ear, let him hear what the Spirit saith unto the churches; To him that overcometh will I give to eat of the hidden manna, and will give him a white stone, and in the stone a new name written, which no man knoweth saving he that receiveth it.

And he that overcometh, and keepeth my works unto the end, to him will I give power over the nations:

³He that overcometh, the same shall be clothed in white raiment; and I will not blot out his name out of the book of life, but I will confess his name before my Father, and before his angels.

Him that overcometh will I make a pillar in the temple of my God, and he shall go no more out: and I will write upon him the name of my God, and the name of the city of my God, which is new Jerusalem, which cometh down out of heaven from my God: and I will write upon him my new name.

To him that overcometh will I grant to sit with me in my throne, even as I also overcame, and am set down with my Father in his throne.

He that overcometh shall inherit all things; and I will be his God, and he shall be my son (Revelation 2:7, 17, 26, 3:5, 12, 21, 21:7).

The phrases *he that has an ear* and *he that overcomes* appeared severally in the Book of Revelation. So what does it mean to hear? Who are these that will overcome? What and who will they overcome? Answers to these all-important questions require revelation from God and for these we ought to pray.

To have an ear means to be able spiritually to hear and discern; to understand the source of your information. To some people, they believe that to overcome means to manipulate themselves into the leadership of the church or government and know everyone that matters in the city. To overcome means to them getting anything they want by any means necessary. They think that once they start a church, gather multitudes, build big cathedral and have enough money in their bank accounts, then they have overcome. Wrong.

The devil is ready to collaborate with you to gather multitudes and give you anything on earth at his disposal if he is sure you will not tell people the truth or glorify God. Some ministers enter into covenant with devil to acquire evil force that can push people down in the guise of being under anointing and afterwards rise to their feet with more problems. Others can do anything humanly possible to gather immeasurable material wealth, drive big cars, bewitch people to sow massive seeds and reduce people serving under them to perpetual slaves. These instances do not show you have overcome. Those who truly overcome do overcome sin, Satan, world, flesh and can live to serve God with or without material benefits and under any situation.

'I write unto you, fathers, because ye have known Him that is from the beginning. I write unto you, young men, because ye have overcome the wicked one. I write unto you, little children, because ye have known the Father' (1John 2:13).

'Ye are of God, little children, and have overcome them: because greater is he that is in you, than he that is in the world' (1 John 4:4).

'For whatsoever is born of God overcometh the world: and this is the victory that overcometh the world, even our faith. Who is he that overcometh the world, but he that believeth that Jesus is the Son of God?' (1 John 5:4-5).

Millions of people may be calling you 'daddy,' 'man of God' or any other name of your choice, making you to view yourself as one who has overcome, one that has arrived and the spiritual father to many people.

This is a misconception. In actual sense, to overcome is to know God and His son, Lord Jesus Christ, personally. Such are the ones who have real testimonies of their salvation and undistracted relationship with Christ.

Believers that overcome have great testimonies of faith and consistent Christian life abiding always in Christ. These believers are not in any way covenanted with the wicked one. Though they are in the world but they are not under the influence of the prince of this world, instead they overcome the world. They keep their faith, fight good fight of faith, press forward for the mark of the high calling and earnestly contend to the end under any situation and circumstance.

True believers who overcome are not enticed with fake powers or wealth of fallen ministers, which they parade about to confuse the mind of the simple. A true believer values his or her faith as a priceless treasure that must be guarded until the end and under any circumstance. A true believer ignores the powers from elemental forces and angels that could not keep their estate in heaven (see Jude 1:6-8). A true believer cannot exchange his or her faith with anything, even the whole world, how much less temporary blessings.

In times of distress, true believers that have overcome devil and his works guard their faith. In times of sickness, poverty, lack, mockery, shame and perplexity, they guard their faith firmly. They persevere to the end and never allow threats of evil militants, demonic leaders and their evil policies, fierce opposition, false prophecies and fiery furnace of suffering, hardship and occult grand masters to sweep off their faith in Christ Jesus. Those that overcome the world believe and serve God with all their hearts and strength. They hold fast their faith even in darkest moments when foundations on which the men of the world built their hopes are being ruthlessly swept off.

Do you want to join believers that have overcome, to eat the fruit from the tree of life, which is in the midst of the paradise of God? Do you want to join them to receive power over all nations? Do you want to join them to be clothed with white raiment that your name is not be blotted out of the book of life? Do you want to join believers that have overcome so that Christ will introduce you to His Father and all the angels in heaven? Do you want to join them so that Christ will make you unmovable pillar in the temple of God? Do you want to join them so that you will remain with God forever and live forever in the New Jerusalem, not this present Jerusalem? Do you want to join them so that you will be granted to sit with Christ in His throne with His Father? Do you want to join them so that you can inherit all things and become God's child forever? Then you have chosen the right path.

Every true believer must overcome sin, evil, fear, idolatry and all unrighteousness in this life.

'But the fearful, and unbelieving, and the abominable, and murderers, and whoremongers, and sorcerers, and idolaters, and all liars, shall have their part in the lake, which burns with fire and brimstone: which is the second death' (Revelation 21:8).

The first step you must take is to acknowledge your sins, confess them and ask God to forgive you. Invite Jesus Christ into your life and ask Him to forgive you, empower you by His grace to forsake and live above sin. You can live a holy life if you choose to. Ask God to help you and keep you out of sin all times. It is well with your soul.

CHAPTER THREE

SECOND LETTER - QUALITIES OF A SAVIOR

(Revelation 2:8-11)

The name 'Jesus Christ' is far above every other name in heaven and on earth. The name still speaks to every church today. Jesus walked in the midst of the seven churches in Asia as recorded in the book of Revelation chapters two and three.

'And I turned to see the voice that spake with me. And being turned, I saw seven golden candlesticks; And in the midst of the seven candlesticks one like unto the Son of man, clothed with a garment down to the foot, and girt about the paps with a golden girdle... The mystery of the seven stars which thou sawest in my right hand, and the seven golden candlesticks. The seven stars are the angels of the seven churches: and the seven candlesticks, which thou sawest are the seven churches' (Revelation 1:12-13, 20).

Jesus Christ is the head of His living church. His splendor and power reverberated through the entire Book of Revelation as written here:

'Unto the angel of the church of Ephesus write; These things saith He that holdeth the seven stars in His right hand, who walketh in the midst of the seven golden candlesticks... And unto the angel of the church in Smyrna write; These things saith the first and the last, which was dead, and is alive... And unto the angel of the church in Thyatira write; These things saith the Son of God, who hath His eyes like unto a flame of fire, and His feet are like fine brass' (Revelation 2:1, 8, 18).

Christ speaks to the angels of all living churches together with the ministers, pastors, teachers and overseers. He speaks to them through His Word. If you want to hear Christ speak to you, spend enough time in His Word. You will certainly hear Him speak directly to your heart. Also, if you desire real deliverance from the devil and his agents, listen to God's Word as well; obey His Words and keep His commandments.

His Word is a panacea for far-reaching and enduring deliverance. Therefore, any minister, saint, bishop, shepherd, high priest, pastor, etc., that wishes to experience genuine deliverance must find time to immerse him or herself in God's Word.

No power in heaven and on earth can reverse whatever Jesus does, approve, or confirms. If He confirms your deliverance, the devil, his agents and all your enemies put together cannot change it. You have no need bothering yourself about your problems, enemies and activities of the devil. What God expects from you is to come to Him through Jesus His only begotten Son. If you need deliverance, go to Jesus. If you need prosperity, liberation or anything, meet Jesus. He introduced Himself in the verse below as the Alpha and Omega, the beginning and the end. The immediate promise to you right now is that if you are thirsty, He can quench your thirst and give you anything you want freely.

'And He said unto me, It is done. I am Alpha and Omega, the beginning and the end. I will give unto him that is athirst of the fountain of the water of life freely' (Revelation 21:6).

'Jesus answered and said unto them, Destroy this temple, and in three days I will raise it up. Then said the Jews, Forty and six years was this temple in building, and wilt thou rear it up in three days? But He spake of the temple of His body. When therefore He was risen from the dead, His disciples remembered that He had said this unto them; and they believed the scripture, and the word which Jesus had said' (John 2:19-22).

It is good to pray for deliverance from devil, his agents and problems but one of the more efficient ways to do so is to believe in the written Word of God concerning your deliverance, act on it and your deliverance will manifest. While many will argue that it is not out of place to seek for deliverance through any means that does not contradict the scriptures but if you would remain faithful with God, study His Word, pray and believe in Christ as your Lord and Savior, your deliverance will surely come from Christ directly.

'Therefore doth my Father love me, because I lay down my life, that I might take it again. No man taketh it from me, but I lay it down of myself. I have power to lay it down, and I have power to take it again. This commandment have I received of my Father' (John 10:17-18).

'For I delivered unto you first of all that which I also received, how that Christ died for our sins according to the scriptures; And that He was buried, and that He rose again the third day according to the scriptures' (1 Corinthians 15:3-4).

At the garden of Gethsemane, the devil mobilized his agents to cut short the life of Jesus Christ (*see* Matthew 26:36-68). Hardly did they realize that Jesus laid down His life on His own. The devil and his agents rejoiced over the betrayal, subsequent death and burial of Jesus for three days. Judas used all the witchcraft he knew. He received money, got rich over night by the powers of witchcraft and betrayed Christ. Christ laid down His life and his unfriendly friend, Judas, betrayed Him for the sake of money. How sad!

In this world, it is possible to lose your life, your marriage, business, ministry or even part of your organs to witches, wizards, unfriendly friends and household enemies. Always remember that Christ suffered and lost his life too. Devil, his agents and wicked people attacked Christ. Devil mobilized a band of men and officers from the chief priest and the Pharisees to arrest and humiliate Jesus. They came at night with lanterns, torches and weapons. They took everything away from Him including His ministry. Imagine what it means to suffer such humiliation.

On the day, the band of captains and officers of the Jews who are also His own relatives led Him away in bounds to Anas, the father-in-law to Caiaphas, the high priest.

Before the morning, Peter, James, John and the rest of the disciples had run away and abandoned Christ. Alone in the battlefield of life, those soldiers dealt with Jesus, struck Him with the palms of their hands and Anas bound Him unto Caiaphas the high priest. They took Him from one place to another, and finally, to the judgment hall where Pilate judged Him and condemned Him to death by crucifixion. Christ carried His own cross to a place of skull, called Golgotha and they crucified Him in between two criminals after mocking and humiliating Him. Later, they took His body down from the cross and handed Him over to the powers of the grave and demons in-charge of dead bodies. These demons have never lost a single dead body committed to their care from time immemorial.

Keeping dead bodies intact was an assignment from the devil, the head of the angels that could not keep their estate in heaven; the god of this world and the adversary of brethren. The first and second day passed and the first day of the week came, which was the day of the greatest battle since creation. The devil, his agents and demons in-charge of dead bodies were all aware of what Jesus had said. Jesus had told them that no matter what they did, they would not be able to operate on the third day, the first day of the week. It was an open challenge to the powers of darkness.

On the third day, as heavily built Roman soldiers guarded the grave, something happened. All the powers of darkness with their head, the devil, were there. Witches and wizards were there. Before the altars of darkness and the sepulcher of all sepulchers on earth, where a heavy stone of hindrance was placed on top of the grave, something happened. The linen and grave clothes that bound Christ's hand and foot could no longer perform their purposes. There was a suddenly release of high power from heaven. The earth shook. The Son of God, Jesus Christ of Nazareth, defeated death and rose again to life eternal. Immediately a word went forth:

'He is not here: for He is risen, as He said. Come, see the place where the Lord lay. And go quickly, and tell His disciples that He is risen from the dead; and, behold, He goeth before you into Galilee; there shall ye see Him: lo, I have told you. And they departed quickly from the sepulchre with fear and great joy; and did run to bring His disciples word' (Matthew 28:6-8).

On that day, Mary Magdalene and the other Mary met an empty tomb because there was a release of the power of the resurrection. That power came from the third heaven, entered the grave, quickened Jesus and He that was dead, under the watchful eyes of the dark kingdoms and human agents, rose up gallantly and His glory knocked down the devil, his agents, the Roman soldiers assigned to shoot at sight every moving thing that neared the grave on the third day. As they fell on the ground defeated, Christ, the Alpha and Omega, the beginning and the end, walked out of the grave, marched upon the devil, his agents, the Roman soldiers and walked boldly into Jerusalem. All the dead saints who were dead before Him that were buried and handed over to the grave and demons in-charge of them walked out of their graves and followed Christ to Jerusalem.

I am not against people who say they are untouchable but if you are already touched, do not bother, Christ was touched but not beyond the third day. You have suffered enough and today is your third day, if only you can repent and hand over your case file to Jesus.

If you are not yet born-again, do so now and join the saints because we are going to march out of every problem and bondage. Today is your day of freedom and problems can no longer hold you down. Today, as you repent, you will join fellow saints and march to freedom. No problem, power of darkness, witches and wizards or evil altars will hold you down again. If you are a believer, you are a saint and you will march out from all problems. You have suffered enough and the devil knows that. Your deliverance from the devil and his agents is now. No more postponement, no more delay, enough is enough. No shrine, no altar, no witch or wizard will hold you down to bondage again. As it is written:

As a sinner, a Christian, you may have killed someone few minutes ago or committed abortion few days ago. Nevertheless, you are now brought close by the blood of Jesus, you are no longer a stranger, foreigner but a fellow citizen with the saints. This a great mystery.

'But now in Christ Jesus ye who sometimes were far off are made nigh by the blood of Christ... Now therefore ye are no more strangers and foreigners, but fellow citizens with the saints, and of the household of God' (Ephesians 2:13, 19).

You have a right to deliverance through the blood of Jesus. You have right to be free, liberated from the devil and his agents. Jesus laid down His life. Satan assumed the position, manipulated his agents to betray and kill Jesus. He made sure the body of Jesus was handed over to the grave. But on the third day, Jesus defeated death and the grave and took away their powers.

You may have handed over your destiny to an occult or witchcraft group, an evil altar or even to the devil, himself. They may have eaten up your marriage, destroyed your womb and every organ of your body. They may even have buried your destiny and handed you over to the grave. This message is for you - Jesus is calling you to come to Him.

'Come unto me, all ye that labour and are heavy laden, and I will give you rest. Take my yoke upon you, and learn of me; for I am meek and lowly in heart: and ye shall find rest unto your souls. For my yoke is easy, and my burden is light' (Matthew 11:28-30).

Open your mouth now and talk to Jesus in prayer. Tell Him all that you need, tell Him to deliver you from the devil, his agents and problems.

He laid down His life and He took it back for your sake. He can deliver you right now.

> 'For I verily, as absent in body, but present in spirit, have judged already, as though I were present, concerning him that hath so done this deed, In the name of our Lord Jesus Christ, when ye are gathered together, and my spirit, with the power of our Lord Jesus Christ' (1 Corinthians 15:3-4).

> 'Him, being delivered by the determinate counsel and foreknowledge of God, ye have taken, and by wicked hands have crucified and slain: Whom God hath raised up, having loosed the pains of death: because it was not possible that he should be holden of it' (Acts 2:23-24).

If you are a sinner, confess your sins now and ask Jesus to forgive you. He died so that if you repent and ask for forgiveness, you will be forgiven. If you are under the torment of wicked hands, Christ was delivered into the hands of more wicked people than the ones tormenting you now. He can deliver you from death.

He can raise you from death and loose you from pains of death. If death could not hold Him, the same death cannot hold those who handed their lives to Him. You can go to Him right now, ask Him to deliver you, set you free and give you abundant life. He will never let you down.

'But ye denied the Holy One and the Just, and desired a murderer to be granted unto you; And killed the Prince of life, whom God hath raised from the dead; whereof we are witnesses' (Acts 3:14-15).

'And we are witnesses of all things which he did both in the land of the Jews, and in Jerusalem; whom they slew and hanged on a tree: Him God raised up the third day, and shewed him openly; Not to all the people, but unto witnesses chosen before of God, even to us, who did eat and drink with him after he rose from the dead' (Acts 10:39-41).

Jesus delivered the church in Ephesus and today, He is still delivering His own. Come! You can obtain your deliverance instantly. It is erroneous to believe that there is bondage Jesus cannot break. It is wrong to believe there is a strongman Jesus cannot bring down to set you free. It is wrong to believe that your foundation or wicked people around you are very powerful. Are they more powerful than murderers that crucified Christ?

Ancestral bondage, wicked people around you and witches and wizards attacking you cannot be wicked than a generation of people that demanded the death of Christ but desired that a murderer be set free. Are your enemies more ferocious than Judas, who betrayed Christ? Problems and wicked people in your place, city or nation cannot be as wicked as the people that killed the prince of life. The good news is that if they could not hold the prince of life who is in-charge of all lives, then they will not hold yours because the prince of life will save, deliver and set free every other life in His care. The witches slew and hanged Him on the tree, but God raised Him. No matter where they have hanged your marriage, business, womb, destiny and all your blessings, God will deliver it today. This should be our message always, as Paul the Apostle went about sharing the gospel of Christ:

'And Paul, as his manner was, went in unto them, and three Sabbath days reasoned with them out of the scriptures, Opening and alleging, that Christ must needs have suffered, and risen again from the dead; and that this Jesus, whom I preach unto you, is Christ' (Acts 17:2-3).

'Who was delivered for our offences, and was raised again for our justification' (Romans 4:25).

Quit complaining that you are suffering too much or you are under heavy attack by enemies. Often, what you are passing through could be a great testimony that you cannot afford to allow pass you by. If Christ did not suffer and die, would He have had any need to be raised to glory? What if present sufferings are meant to strengthen your endurance so you can preach to others about deliverance and Christ's power to deliver? One thing that is worth learning is that the world needs a deliverer, Savior and redeemer. Christ laid down His life for the sake of our sins. He was raised again for our justification. The whole world needs salvation through Christ Jesus.

If deliverance does not lead you to know Christ, preach Him and serve Him, your deliverance may be fake deliverance. That is why I disagree with many deliverance ministries and ministers that conduct deliverances without any substance. Paul was delivered to know Christ, live for Him, serve Him and die for His sake. When you see anyone who testifies that Christ delivered him and yet goes back to sin or practices sin, his deliverance is fake one. Deliverance ministers who deliver others but live in sin are fake and their deliverances are fake and temporary. You shall know them by their fruits.

When you confess with your mouth the Lord Jesus Christ, the next thing that must follow your confession is salvation. Apart from that, your confession is incomplete and your faith is shallow. Every testimony of deliverance from poverty, witchcraft attacks and all enemies without salvation and freedom from sin is incomplete and temporary.

'That if thou shalt confess with thy mouth the Lord Jesus, and shalt believe in thine heart that God hath raised him from the dead, thou shalt be saved' (Romans 10:9).

'Which he wrought in Christ, when he raised him from the dead, and set him at his own right hand in the heavenly places' (Ephesians 1:20).

What happened when God raised Jesus Christ from the dead is more than material blessings. It is far above physical blessings and earthly possessions. It is far above all the good things on earth put together. As a matter of fact, when devil sees you jumping up and down, testifying of your deliverance from witchcraft powers without salvation, he laughs at you.

Another important aspect of deliverance is your primary motive for seeking deliverance. If your only motive for deliverance is so that you could enjoy material and physical blessings like every other person, then you are uninformed. Your primary motive for seeking deliverance should so that you may know Christ more, experience His power of salvation here on earth and escape the reality of eternal death in hell. This motive is enough to get any true Christian concerned. Sadly, most Christian are seeking deliverance from devil and all his works. Jesus said,

'Fear not them which kill the body, but are not able to kill the soul: but rather fear him which is able to destroy both soul and body in hell' (Matthew 10:28).

Jesus who wrote to the seven churches in Asia has the most intimate knowledge of all that pertains to the churches. He is the first and the last. He knows that many deliverance ministers, ministries and pastors in the seven Asian churches are not informed. Churches were filled with deliverance ministers who were not delivered, pastors who were not trained and ministers who have not been ministered to.

Today, we are privileged that Jesus our Savior is the greatest deliverance minister, the bishop of all bishops and He was there when the foundation of the earth is being laid. Let us go to Him for our personal or direct relationship and complete deliverance because He knows every church in every age and time as revealed here, please read:

I know thy works, and thy labour, and thy patience, and how thou canst not bear them which are evil: and thou hast tried them which say they are apostles, and are not, and hast found them liars:

I know thy works, and tribulation, and poverty, (but thou art rich) and I know the blasphemy of them which say they are Jews, and are not, but are the synagogue of Satan.

I know thy works, and where thou dwellest, even where Satan's seat is: and thou holdest fast my name, and hast not denied my faith, even in those days wherein Antipas was my faithful martyr, who was slain among you, where Satan dwelleth.

I know thy works, and charity, and service, and faith, and thy patience, and thy works; and the last to be more than the first' (Revelation 2:2, 9, 13, 19).

And unto the angel of the church in Sardis write; These things saith he that hath the seven Spirits of God, and the seven stars; I know thy works, that thou hast a name that thou livest, and art dead.

I know thy works: behold, I have set before thee an open door, and no man can shut it: for thou hast a little strength, and hast kept my word, and hast not denied my name.

I know thy works, that thou art neither cold nor hot: I would thou wert cold or hot' (Revelation 3:1, 8, 15).

Jesus Christ remains the only true authority. So, when men, pastors, deliverance ministers, doctors in developed and underdeveloped worlds have done their all and there is nothing left they could do, Jesus is the answer. Let us go to Him for personal deliverances. He said to the church in Ephesus, I know your works.

'I know thy works, and tribulation, and poverty, (but thou art rich) and I know the blasphemy of them which say they are Jews, and are not, but are the synagogue of Satan' (Revelation 2:9).

He is still talking to His church today. Are you not tired of going up and down? Let us go to the one that knows all. He wrote to the church in Smyrna, so let us see the monuments and Smyrna's antiquities.

THE MONUMENTS OF SMYRNA

We are going to see the national monument of Smyrna; effigies, potential signs and landmarks of the city that received one of the seven letters. Smyrna was a city in Asia that existed before the middle ages in ancient times. It had a long history and was founded before Christ as a Greek colony.

Founded 11th century B C by the Aeolians, a Greek people, the city was seized by the Ionians before 688 B C. Later in the 7th century BC, the Lydians, a people of Asia Minor, devastated Smyrna. Antigonus I, king of Macedonia, restored the city in the 4th century BC, and subsequently it was fortified and improved by Lysimachus, a general in the service of Alexander the Great. Smyrna was conquered later by the Romans and subsequently became an early center of Christianity, referred to as one of the "seven churches" (*see* Revelation 1:11).

Smyrna regained its Greek characteristics in the third century B.C. Because of its excellent harbor, Smyrna retained its importance and it is today a large commercial city, through which they trade to and from the interior of Asia Minor passes. Later, Jesus would write to the church in Smyrna -

> '...*I am Alpha and Omega, the first and the last: and, What thou seest, write in a book, and send it unto the seven churches which are in Asia; unto Ephesus, and unto Smyrna, and unto Pergamos, and unto Thyatira, and unto Sardis, and unto Philadelphia, and unto Laodicea*' (Revelation 1:11).

'And unto the angel of the church in Smyrna write; These things saith the first and the last, which was dead, and is alive' (Revelation 2:8).

At the time Christ sent this message to the angels of the church in Smyrna, the city was the center for Emperor's Worship. Smyrna was a pagan society with idols hung on every side of the road as electric poles would line up along the road. Idolatry was commercialized and anyone who was not an idol worshipper was seen as a strange person. At that time, believers were under persecution, in fierce and profound hardship enduring untold trials and tribulations.

'I know thy works, and tribulation, and poverty, (but thou art rich) and I know the blasphemy of them which say they are Jews, and are not, but are the synagogue of Satan. Fear none of those things which thou shalt suffer: behold, the devil shall cast some of you into prison, that ye may be tried; and ye shall have tribulation ten days: be thou faithful unto death, and I will give thee a crown of life' (Revelation 2:9-10).

'If the world hates you, ye know that it hated me before it hated you. If ye were of the world, the world would love his own: but because ye are not of the world, but I have chosen you out of the world, therefore the world hateth you' (John 15:18-19).

The church in Smyrna was a suffering church, filled with poor members, pastors and ministers. Their persecutors were motivated by the devil who recruited evil men to destroy their faith in Christ. Most religious people in the city of Smyrna who called 'God or Lord' were also involved in cultism. Religious Jews who claimed to observe Mosaic laws were devil incarnates, witches and wizards, just like many evil godfathers in many churches today. So many religious leaders like bishops, reverends, priests and archbishops who claimed to worship God are all devil incarnates, evil principalities and synagogue of Satan those days. Most religious leaders, church founders, general overseers and prophets who controlled big crowds, except few, blasphemed against God.

An encounter with some famous religious leaders in today's churches will prove to you that most of them have direct contact with the devil. Leaving them and their so-called churches is more difficult than leaving local Ogboni[8] cult in Nigeria. They are very dangerous and destructive. Jesus wrote to the church in Smyrna that He knows their works; tribulations, poverty and all that they were going through.

Many people in churches today have had their business, marriage, health and ministry suffer enormously because of their encounters with occult ministers who operate synagogues of devil. Others are poor, weak, sick, and unable to pay house rents, train their children, live

---

[8] *A secret confraternity in the Southern part of Nigeria*

comfortable lives and enjoy the Christian life because of these evil ministers. So many gatherings in many so-called churches today are worse than the gathering of witches.

Each day in fellowship, we are reminded of recurring incidences of members losing parts of their destinies, joy and peace in churches. Yet they cannot leave because of fear of attacks from evil ministers of such churches. When Christ saw what believers in Smyrna were going through, He wrote and encouraged them not to be afraid anymore.

Today, I decree and declare that your fears will begin to fear you. This is the time to break out from every yoke of limitation, bondage and satanic blockades. They may have bewitched others, destroyed peoples' lives, marriages, businesses and wasted destinies, but that was yesterday, last week, last month and yester years. Today, as you read this letter from Christ, the failure of your enemies will start and your deliverance will begin. The church in Smyrna was attacked by devil through his agents who rendered many of them poor and wretched while imprisoning their joy, peace, success and breakthroughs. It will not continue after going through this deliverance. You will be delivered from the devil and all his agents, in the mighty name of Jesus.

The persecution you are experiencing now may increase but do not be afraid. Remain faithful to God. You may need to suffer a little but never give up. Do not backslide or compromise. Rejections, hatred and attacks may increase, but do not surrender. God is working out your deliverance and complete freedom from the devil and all his agents. Be encouraged by these verses -

'Moreover, brethren, we do you to wit of the grace of God bestowed on the churches of Macedonia; How that in a great trial of affliction the abundance of their joy and their deep poverty abounded unto the riches of their liberality. For to their power, I bear record, yea, and beyond their power, they were willing of themselves; praying us with much intreaty that we would receive the gift, and take upon us the fellowship of the ministering to the saints. And this they did, not as we hoped, but first gave their own selves to the Lord, and unto us by the will of God' (2 Corinthians 8:1-5).

'But we desire to hear of thee what thou thinkest: for as concerning this sect, we know that everywhere it is spoken against' (Acts 28:22).

The letter you are reading today, sent to the church in Smyrna says, 'Fear not!' It is but for a short while. Strongmen, witches and wizards around you may be posing as moving altars, but fear them not. Every other person you know may be entering into one evil group or the other to avoid being attacked, but do not be moved. Do not join them but remain faithful to Christ and serve God. Do not touch any money or gift that is offered to idols no matter how needy you may be. If you must go to any gathering, occasion or family meeting and you are led to drink, eat and dine with them, you are free to do so but be wise.

Whatever you do, do it to the glory of God and not against your conscience. Learn how to pray, bless with strong mind. Eat if the Spirit leads you. Almost everything sold in Smyrna at that time was first offered unto idols before they took them to the market. Our world today is not different. Therefore, you cannot avoid everything and everyone. Better to learn how to bless and commit everything to God especially what is going into your belly. Read this:

A poor woman once called a Christian radio station asking for assistance. A Satanist listening to the radio program decided to shame the woman and make her to realize that good things do not come from GOD. He called his secretary to buy food and take to the woman that called for assistance. He said to his secretary, 'If she asks who sent the food, tell her it's from the devil.'

The woman was so happy to receive the food. The secretary then asked, 'Wouldn't you want to know who sent you the food?' The woman answered, 'No my dear, it does not matter. When God orders even the devil obeys.'

May God order even your enemies to obey and serve you forever, in the name of Jesus. Wherever you are whether in the office, home, market, school and public places, always be confident to take a stand for Christ. Before the world pulls you over, pull the world to Christ. If you cannot convince anyone, convince yourself and stay with Christ. Believers and the church in Smyrna took their stand and Christ commended them. Let Christ commend you today, in your school, community, office, market and everywhere you are now.

The world may call you old fashion or outdated brother or sister, but that should not be a problem because what Christ calls you is much better than what the world calls you. They may despise you, victimize you, tease you or persecute you, but do not be afraid. They also called

Paul a pestilent fellow and mover of sedition, a ringleader of the sect of the Nazarenes.

> 'For we have found this man a pestilent fellow, and a mover of sedition among all the Jews throughout the world, and a ringleader of the sect of the Nazarenes' (*Acts 24:5*).

> 'But the Jews stirred up the devout and honorable women, and the chief men of the city, and raised persecution against Paul and Barnabas, and expelled them out of their coasts' (*Acts 13:50*).

Any name they call you for Christ's sake is better than any name the world would call you. The world may expel you, persecute you, avoid and deny you of your rights, benefits and entitlements, pray to God and report them to Him. Take the case file to the Almighty God. He will deliver you from devil and his agents.

> 'But the unbelieving Jews stirred up the Gentiles, and made their minds evil affected against the brethren' (*Acts 14:2*).

> 'And when there was an assault made both of the Gentiles, and also of the Jews with their rulers, to use them despitefully, and to stone them' (*Acts 14:5*).

> 'And there came thither certain Jews from Antioch and Iconium, who persuaded the people, and, having stoned

Paul, drew him out of the city, supposing he had been dead' (*Acts 14:19*).

'*But the Jews which believed not, moved with envy, took unto them certain lewd fellows of the baser sort, and gathered a company, and set all the city on an uproar, and assaulted the house of Jason, and sought to bring them out to the people'* (*Acts 17:5*).

'*And when he was come unto us, he took Paul's girdle, and bound his own hands and feet, and said, Thus saith the Holy Ghost, So shall the Jews at Jerusalem bind the man that owneth this girdle, and shall deliver him into the hands of the Gentiles'* (*Acts 21:11*).

Fellow believers or workers in the church may oppose you for loving Jesus so much. Do not give up on your love for Christ. They may even accuse you falsely, talk bad about you or try to take your position in the church, but do not be bothered for no man can take away your name from the book of life.

Many years ago, the devil raised witchcraft crusade against me wherever I go to preach the gospel. Evil revivalist and their agents would accuse me of immorality to discredit my person. This disturbed me so much as I always tried to defend myself. But later, God spoke to me and advised me not to bother because people talk always. My part is to make sure that I am not guilty of whatever people are accusing me of. Thanks to God that time and truth vindicated me. Up until today, some people, including some close friends, still believed that I was complicit. What is important always is the truth because it always prevails.

Some people can persuade a whole church to believe some wicked lies against you, including the pastor. Your part is to make sure whatever they are alleging against you is not true. If they allege that you stole, let it be only a lie against you. If they said that you committed immorality, let it not be true. If they allege that you are a witch, wizard, sinner, husband snatcher, armed robber, occultist, fraudster, confusionist, etc., let all be lies before God and man. God may not stop them from accusing you but they cannot stop God from blessing, promoting or delivering you at the appointed time, am a living witness.

Envious enemies may be able to instigate a rebellion against you, charge you to court and imprison you. But they cannot stop God from releasing you, positioning and delivering you to rise above all your enemies. Prophets may prophesy about your problem, troubles and do many bad things against you, but none can stop God when He comes to deliver you from any bondage.

When Jesus wrote to the church in Smyrna and asked them not to fear, He wanted them to rise above their tribulations, sufferings and problems fearlessly. In this life, troubles, sufferings and challenges are unavoidable and it is normal that believers must pass through them.

'It is a faithful saying: For if we be dead with him, we shall also live with him: If we suffer, we shall also reign with him: if we deny him, he also will deny us' (2 Timothy 2:11-12).

When it is obvious that you must pass through the Red Sea or face any giant like Goliath, then there is no need to listen to even God's prophets trying to persuade you to avoid your battle. God is able to deliver you before you get into a burning fire or lion's den but if God decides to deliver you right inside a burning fire or in the den of lions, do not be afraid.

'And what shall I more say? For the time would fail me to tell of Gedeon, and of Barak, and of Samson, and of Jephthae; of David also, and Samuel, and of the prophets: Who through faith subdued kingdoms, wrought righteousness, obtained promises, stopped the mouths of lions, quenched the violence of fire, escaped the edge of the sword, out of weakness were made strong, waxed valiant in fight, turned to flight the armies of the aliens. Women received their dead raised to life again: and others were tortured, not accepting deliverance; that they might obtain a better resurrection: And others had trial of cruel mockings and scourgings, yea, moreover of bonds and imprisonment: They were stoned, they were sawn asunder, were tempted, were slain with the sword: they wandered about in sheepskins and goatskins; being destitute, afflicted, tormented; (of whom the world was not worthy:) they wandered in deserts, and in mountains, and in dens and caves of the earth' (Hebrews 11:32-38).

The church in Smyrna was a suffering church and Jesus commended them. It did not matter whether the world condemned them, the Jews cursed them or they are cast in prison by persecutors. At the time they received the letter, the storm of persecution was beating fiercely on them because they dared to defy their pagan rulers. They persevered to the end in the midst of poverty.

Though Smyrna was a wealthy city, where buying, selling and getting gain was the all-absorbing occupation, true believers refused to compromise in their businesses. They were poor because of their Christian stance against sin, idolatry and evil ways of doing business in their days. Their unbelieving relatives, friends and rich people around them despised, slandered and insulted them but they stood their grounds and maintained their faith. The government of their day accused them of sedition and disloyalty because of their persistent refusal to offer sacrifices to the emperor. The society denounced them as haters of human race for standing aloof from corrupt practices, popular games, festivals and social gatherings, which frequently involved sacrifices to idols. The Jews also persecuted them regarding them as a sect. Ironically, Jesus saw compromised Jews and backslidden believers as evil people, blasphemers, slanderers, synagogues of Satan and evil assemble of backsliders.

Jesus refers to many church leaders who have given up on God and followed Satan for evil powers as generation of vipers because they are capable of doing so much evil to their members. They love to speak evil of anointed ministers of God. If you ever get closer to them, discover their secrets and try to help to restore them, they will bite you and afflict you with serpentine venom. Indeed, they are serpents and generation of vipers.

'But when he saw many of the Pharisees and Sadducees come to his baptism, he said unto them, O generation of vipers, who hath warned you to flee from the wrath to come?' (Matthew 3:7).

'O generation of vipers, how can ye, being evil, speak good things? For out of the abundance of the heart the mouth speaketh' (Matthew 12:34).

'Ye serpents, ye generation of vipers, how can ye escape the damnation of hell?' (Matthew 23:33).

'Ye are of your father the devil, and the lusts of your father ye will do. He was a murderer from the beginning, and abode not in the truth, because there is no truth in him. When he speaketh a lie, he speaketh of his own: for he is a liar, and the father of it' (John 8:44).

'Which was with the deputy of the country, Sergius Paulus, a prudent man; who called for Barnabas and Saul, and desired to hear the word of God. But Elymas the sorcerer (for so is his name by interpretation) withstood them, seeking to turn away the deputy from the faith. Then Saul, (who also is called Paul,) filled with the Holy Ghost, set his eyes on him, And said, O full of all subtilty and all mischief, thou child of the devil, thou enemy of all righteousness, wilt thou not cease to pervert the right ways of the Lord?' (Acts 13:7-10).

They are the sons of the devil because in times of receiving evil powers, they made the devil their father. They went into covenant with the devil because they coveted the things of this world from the gods of this world and got it with the condition to be a murderer like their father. They were not told the whole truth. The devil deceived them and anointed them to deceive others, their followers and those who discover their secrets and threaten to oppose them. With evil powers, they manipulate governments, leaders, governors and their deputies, Presidents and people in authority to get whatever they want. They get lands, buildings, money and every good thing with curses on them.

'In this the children of God are manifest, and the children of the devil: whosoever doeth not righteousness is not of God, neither he that loveth not his brother' (1 John 3:10).

The good news is Christ's promise of deliverance from the devil and his agents. Only Jesus can deliver you today.

Solemn Admonition From Christ

The church in Smyrna received a friendly counsel from Jesus Christ. What a blessed assurance to know that Jesus is with you always. Jesus admonished them,

> *'Fear none of those things which thou shalt suffer: behold, the devil shall cast some of you into prison, that ye may be tried; and ye shall have tribulation ten days: be thou faithful unto death, and I will give thee a crown of life' (<u>Revelation 2:10</u>).*

> *'And the LORD appeared unto him the same night, and said, I am the God of Abraham thy father: fear not, for I am with thee, and will bless thee, and multiply thy seed for my servant Abraham's sake' (<u>Genesis 26:24</u>).*

That is why you need to always encourage yourself in the LORD your God. Whatever you are going through as a child of God, do not be afraid and do not look back. Do not think of giving up on Jesus or resign your commitment to Him. The church in Smyrna has gone through the same trials, troubles and came out of it victorious. You will come out of your own trials victorious if you would endure for a while. Your trials and suffering cannot last forever. Christ is saying to you today, 'Endure for a little season.'

The woman of Zarephath was never afraid of death. She had strength to prepare her last meal before she and her only son could die while resisting Ahab and Jezebel's witchcrafts. The hunger was severe but God sustained her. She could have witnessed many people die for their faith. She had attended many burial ceremonies and she was ready to die also instead of compromising her faith.

'And Elijah said unto her, Fear not; go and do as thou hast said: but make me thereof a little cake first, and bring it unto me, and after make for thee and for thy son' (1 Kings 17:13).

'And he answered, Fear not: for they that be with us are more than they that be with them' (2 Kings 6:16).

'Fear thou not; for I am with thee: be not dismayed; for I am thy God: I will strengthen thee; yea, I will help thee; yea, I will uphold thee with the right hand of my righteousness' (Isaiah 41:10).

Ahab and Jezebel's witchcraft was not a threat to her. Death had already killed many of her friends and relatives. Therefore, she was no longer afraid. She lived and contended to the day Elisha visited her and told her to fear not. Today, you are alive like the church in Smyrna hearing not from Elijah, Ahab or any rich man in the world but from Christ. Jesus is saying to you today, 'Do not be afraid.' Whatever hunger has done to you and your family, fear not. Christ is telling you today to stop being afraid of evil things you know the devil can do.

Elijah's message to the woman of Zarephath was 'fear not, go and do as thou hast said, the barrel of meal shall not waste, neither shall the cruse of oil fail, according to the word of the Lord, which he spoke by Elijah (*see* 1 Kings 17:13-14). Whatever your problem is, whether it is cancer, fibroid, barrenness, demonic attacks or threats from ferocious witches, Christ is telling you today, 'Fear none of those things.'

Jesus told the church at Smyrna to stop being afraid of the occult grandmasters, poverty and the devil. Today is your time to receive the Words of Jesus. He is able to deliver you from the devil, all his agents and problems. Your house rent may be due for renewal; the landlord may be knocking at your door at this moment, the medical reports may be negative but Christ has the final say. Fear not!

You may have woke up today with pains, burden, problems and great enemies, but fear not. A host of soldiers with horses and chariots, who had a mandate to arrest Elisha, surrounded him. But he did not fear them. I cannot tell the kind of negative circumstances that are surrounding you right now and threatening to kill you. But this is an assurance from Jesus, the lion of the tribe of Judah, the Alpha and the Omega. He is saying to you, 'Fear not.' Elisha told his servant, 'fear not; for they that are with us are more than they that are with them' (2 Kings 6:16).

The letter Jesus sent to the church in Smyrna is not strictly for them only. Today is your time to share in the abundance of this message. Read it through and believe in what Jesus is saying. The bible is filled with great admonitions and encouragement from God. It is a manual of deliverance from above. In the day of Isaiah, he confronted enemies greater than the ones you have today. How did he overcome them? He read God's Word and trusted God.

God's Word is written for our learning and deliverance from the devil and his agents together with the problems of life. God told Isaiah, '*Fear thou not; for I am with thee: be not dismayed; for I am thy God: I will strengthen thee; yea, I will help thee; yea, I will uphold thee with the right hand of my righteousness*' (Isaiah 41:10).

The truth is that we are privileged today more than believers in Smyrna, the woman of Zarephath and Old Testament saints. Why? They received only one letter, believed it and they were delivered from all their problems. But today, all the letters of deliverance from Genesis to Revelation are given to us free of charge. Therefore, I encourage you to read them, believe them and claim the promises therein. It is well with you and your family.

If you are a true believer, it would be hard for you to listen to people that would tell you that anything is impossible. With God, nothing is impossible. It is better to believe in Christ and all the letters of deliverance in the bible instead of your problems.

If you are looking for what to believe, open the scriptures. Do not allow negative things, problems and empty voices around you to lure you into believing in lies of the devil. Are you ready to listen to God, the creator Lord that created you? If your answer is yes, then here is a wonderful passage to encourage you:

'*But now thus saith the LORD that created thee, O Jacob, and he that formed thee, O Israel, Fear not: for I have redeemed thee, I have called thee by thy name; thou art mine. When thou passest through the waters, I will be with thee;*

and through the rivers, they shall not overflow thee: when thou walkest through the fire, thou shalt not be burned; neither shall the flame kindle upon thee. For I am the LORD thy God, the Holy One of Israel, thy Saviour: I gave Egypt for thy ransom, Ethiopia and Seba for thee' (Isaiah 43:1-3).

'But the very hairs of your head are all numbered. Fear ye not therefore, ye are of more value than many sparrows' (Matthew 10:30-31).

The same Word God gave to Isaiah, He is giving to you today - Fear not, I have redeemed you, called you by your name, you are mine. If God said you should not be afraid, who or what in the world would then make you afraid? If God said that He has redeemed you, who is able to return you to bondage? If God said you are His property, child, that means that even death cannot claim you unless you decide to hand yourself over to death free of charge.

Child of God, whatever you are passing through now, God said He would be with you. If God is with you, water spirits and their wickedness will flee before God. Evil cannot enter your life from your village river. If your enemies like let them offer one million sacrifices to the queen of the coast, but they cannot flow into your life. If they like let them call their gods, evil spirits like the prophets of Baal from morning to night, they cannot touch you. If your enemies like let them sleep in seven altars, enter one million cults, call fires of death, but they shall not burn you. If they like let them inflame occult fires around your house, office, shops or rooftop. The reality is that such evil flames have no power over you. Why? Because you have a God; the Holy One of Israel. He dealt with Pharaoh of Egypt and He is able to deal with your wicked enemies.

The hairs of your head are numbered and you are of more valuable than many sparrows. If you refuse to give up on God, the church of Christ and insist for your deliverance, you will be fully delivered in due time. If you refuse to visit evil altars, no power can keep you in bondage. If you would embrace the Word of God believing His instructions, admonitions and counsels, you will be delivered from the devil, his agents and all their problems. God is saying to you today:

'Fear not, little flock; for it is your Father's good pleasure to give you the kingdom' (Luke 12:32).

'And now, behold, I go bound in the spirit unto Jerusalem, not knowing the things that shall befall me there: Save that the Holy Ghost witnesseth in every city, saying that bonds and afflictions abide me. But none of these things move me, neither count I my life dear unto myself, so that I might finish my course with joy, and the ministry, which I have received of the Lord Jesus, to testify the gospel of the grace of God' (Acts 20:22-24).

You are God's little flock and it is your Father's good pleasure to give you not only deliverance here on earth but His kingdom in heaven. The enemy may have taken over you, bound you spiritually and carried you away far into their kingdom. God has promised to deliver you. They may have taken you away from all your helpers, destroyed your flesh, shared your destiny in the witchcraft coven, but God said He will deliver you. Therefore, trust in the LORD your God with all your heart.

No matter how poor you are or how strong your enemies are, God will surely deliver you. You may not know how God would deliver you or where His help would come from. That should not be your worry. What you need to do is to embrace His Word of promise and deliverance. That was what believers in Smyrna did. The woman of Zarephath and others did the same. Prophets in our time may prophesy negative things concerning you; doctors may deliver their death verdicts but trust in the LORD with all your heart. That was what happened to Hezekiah but he prayed, reminded God of His promise of freedom, and deliverance and God delivered him from death.

Paul faced similar circumstances but all his enemies surrendered in the end. You may need to get a copy of one of my books titled *21/40 Nights of Decrees and Your Enemies will Surrender*. When Paul was about to go to Jerusalem, many negative voices rose up against him. True prophets at the time were prophesying against his proposed journeys but none of those prophecies moved him. All he decided was to focus on his calling and the mandate Jesus gave to him. God delivered him. He feared none of those things prophesied against him.

Whatever trouble or problem you find yourself in now is a brief, passing and temporary one. It will be over in a little while. Storms may be severe. But it will be short if you would fix your gaze on Jesus. It could be death, but remember that Christ has taken away the stings of death and we may no longer die for nothing. Even at the point of death, be faithful and steadfast. If it is to bear a cross, endure to the end. Carry the cross and follow Jesus. If it is trial in the face of deceits and betrayals of this world, believe God and ignore every distraction. Keep the faith, which is the only thing that Christ requires from you. The battle is about to end. There is a sweet assurance and blessed hope waiting for you ahead. Be strong!

BLESSED HOPE FROM CHRIST

The major reason Jesus commended the church at Smyrna was for their passionate determination and commitment to the truth, true worship and faithfulness unto death. He assured them of his support, deliverance and crown of life. In His words, He said,

'I know thy works, and tribulation, and poverty, (but thou art rich) and I know the blasphemy of them which say they are Jews, and are not, but are the synagogue of Satan' (Revelation 2:9).

'Fear none of those things which thou shalt suffer: behold, the devil shall cast some of you into prison, that ye may be tried; and ye shall have tribulation ten days: be thou faithful unto death, and I will give thee a crown of life. He that hath an ear, let him hear what the Spirit saith unto the churches; He that overcometh shall not be hurt of the second death' (Revelation 2:10-11).

James also put it this way -

'Hearken, my beloved brethren, Hath not God chosen the poor of this world rich in faith, and heirs of the kingdom which he hath promised to them that love him?' (James 2:5)

The omniscient Lord of lords assured the church in Smyrna of His richness because of their faith in Christ even in their poverty. This speaks volume of the genuineness of their faith, love and spiritual life.

They were poor physically but rich in the favor and love of God. They had little material things but were very rich in the gift of the Holy Ghost and knowledge in the things of God. They were rich in consolation and hope in Christ. God choose the poor of this world to be rich in faith and to become heirs of His kingdom. The church in Smyrna was sure of God's promise because they loved God.

If you would endure to the end by following Christ all the way even in times of hardship, He will surely enrich you. Jesus will bless you with right utterances, wisdom and knowledge from above as it is written:

> 'That in everything ye are enriched by Him, in all utterance, and in all knowledge; Even as the testimony of Christ was confirmed in you: So that ye come behind in no gift; waiting for the coming of our Lord Jesus Christ' (*1 Corinthians 1:5-7*).

> 'And every man that striveth for the mastery is temperate in all things. Now they do it to obtain a corruptible crown; but we an incorruptible' (*1 Corinthians 9:25*).

With these, you will no longer lack anything. Your gifts, talents and testimonies will not be in vain. Jesus will bear witness to them. In the end, when you would have fulfilled your purpose on earth, you will make heaven and inherit all things according to God's promises. You will obtain an incorruptible crown. Paul put it this way -

'I have fought a good fight, I have finished my course, I have kept the faith: Henceforth there is laid up for me a crown of righteousness, which the Lord, the righteous judge, shall give me at that day: and not to me only, but unto all them also that love his appearing' (2 Timothy 4:7-8).

'Blessed is the man that endureth temptation: for when he is tried, he shall receive the crown of life, which the Lord hath promised to them that love him' (James 1:12).

Paul is an example of one who made it and received a blessed hope. He fought a good fight of faith, finished his course and kept his faith. The sweet assurance from Christ to the saints in Smyrna is that if they could continue in their faith to the end, they would not regret it. Paul saw the revelation of the glory of God upon him at the end of his life and that was why he did not give up.

Christ could have seen that some believers in Smyrna were about to give up. If that is your situation now, please dear child of God, do not give up. There is a crown laid down for you at the end of your trial. There is a deliverance attached to every problem and satanic attacks you are facing. Jesus will not watch you suffer in vain or without reward. Every battle you have fought, the ones you are fighting and will ever fight for Christ's sake has a crown attached to it. No one has ever followed Christ to the end and failed to be rewarded. You will be rewarded, blessed and fully delivered.

'Behold, I come quickly: hold that fast which thou hast, that no man take thy crown' (Revelation 3:11).

'Blessed and holy is he that hath part in the first resurrection: on such the second death hath no power, but they shall be priests of God and of Christ, and shall reign with him a thousand years.

'And death and hell were cast into the lake of fire. This is the second death.

'And whosoever was not found written in the book of life was cast into the lake of fire' (Revelation 20:6, 14, 15).

Hold onto your faith to the end so that you will not lose the crown of life. You may be helpless now, poor and despised by the people of this world as useless but before Christ, you are rich, cherished and blessed.

Those that overcome will inherit all things according to His promises. These are people that will overcome suffering, oppositions, persecution, and reproach and still not give up. Jesus wants you to overcome your present problems and triumph. Even if any of us should die keeping the faith, nothing has been lost. Any attempt of the enemy to make you deny Christ, reject it even at the point of death. Take a solid stand for Christ always. As there is life beyond the present life, so there is a death beyond the present death. He who is born twice and remains faithful to the end dies only once, but he who is born once, an unbeliever or backslider will die twice.

Therefore, even with threats from Islamic militants, the ISIS and their likes, remain loyal and faithful to Christ to the end. Those that overcome will not have any part in the eternal death, but punishment of the unsaved or backslider is in the lake of fire. Is your name written in the book of life? Have you been born again? If not, do so now, repent of all your sins, confess them, forsake them and embrace Christ. He is the only one that can deliver you from the devil, his agents and all problems of this life. This is the blessed hope and sweet assurance from Christ.

CHAPTER FOUR

THIRD LETTER

PRINCE OF LIFE, SAVIOR AND JUDGE

Revelation 2:12-17

The letter was written because the church in Pergamos bowed in concession to something derogatory or prejudicial. They adjusted and settled wrongly against God's word. In the letter, Christ introduced himself to the church as He that has the SHARP SWORD with two edges.

'And to the angel of the church in Pergamos write; These things saith he which hath the sharp sword with two edges... Repent; or else I will come unto thee quickly, and will fight against them with the sword of my mouth' (Revelation 2:12, 16).

'For the word of God is quick, and powerful, and sharper than any two-edged sword, piercing even to the dividing asunder of soul and spirit, and of the joints and marrow, and is a discerner of the thoughts and intents of the heart' (Hebrews 4:12).

Christ is a prince of life, savior, and prince of peace but can also fight with the sword in His mouth. The believers in Pergamos like many believers today know Christ one sided. They know Christ as extremely merciful, peaceful, kind and compassionate. Many because of such nature take Him for granted and live their lives anyhow. They live discredited lives in mischief without respect or principle. Their way of life brings shame, disrepute to the body of Christ. Their understanding is that Christ is so soft, merciful and cannot harm them. In Christ's letter to such people, He warned them of the consequences. I will come unto thee quickly and will fight against you with the sword of my mouth. The two edges of the sharp sword has two functions. One is to cut away from sin-salvation. The other is to cut off from God eternally- judgment. The same word is the instrument of salvation and judgment.

'And Jesus answered and said unto them, I also will ask you one thing, which if ye tell me, I in likewise will tell you by what authority I do these things' (Matthew 21:44).

'For we are unto God a sweet savor of Christ, in them that are saved, and in them that perish: To the one we are the savor of death unto death; and to the other the savor of life unto life. And who is sufficient for these things?' (2 Corinthians 2:15-16).

142 • Prayer M. Madueke

The truth is that whoever rejects the prince of life, the savior of the world has made a choice, which is judgment. The judgment comes from the same Christ as a result of your decision. The church in Pergamos like many today depend only on God's, grace, mercy, His abundant life and salvation without considering the judgment against compromise. Every sin of compromise has judgment attached to it and unless you repent and forsake sin, you will face the sword of judgment. If you sin and quickly repent, I mean humble yourself, call upon the name of God, pray and seek God's face, turn away from your wicked ways, the sword will cut you away from such sin unto salvation. I don't mean believers who play with sin, sleep with sin and gamble with sin. Believers and unrepentant sinners that the sword will not cut away from sin to salvation are not those who only put embargo on sinful lifestyle only in the church or some places but lift it at home, offices, in hotel rooms, class room and lift it in secrets places. God will not cut you away from sin unto salvation if you lie with sinners, lie by sinners and be with sinners;

'*And Noah went in, and his sons, and his wife, and his sons' wives with him, into the ark, because of the waters of the flood... And it came to pass after seven days, that the waters of the flood were upon the earth*' (*Genesis 39:7, 10*).

For you to be cut away from sin unto salvation, you have to totally refuse sin, wicked acts, flee from sin and suffer for that if need be. It is better to go through any suffering than to be cut off from God eternally. It is better to please God than to please man and displease God. It is better to be condemned by the judges of this world than to be condemned by God. If the judges of this world condemn you because of your obedient to God, Christ will deliver you. But if Christ condemn you, no judge on earth can deliver you. Christ is the stone of every judgment and if you fall on His stone, you shall be broken without remedy. No one survives Christ's judgment because you will be grinded to powder. It is better to face the wrath of man than to compromise with man and face God's wrath. It is better to fight man than to fight God's sword in His mouth, you will not survive it. Christ's letter to the believers in Pergamos is, I give life, save life but I also judge. Sweet salvation comes from Christ for them that are saved but those who despise salvation are judged to perish. You can be cut from death to death and life to life by the same savior. It is wrong, lack of knowledge to understand Christ one sided. The same sword in His mouth is the instrument of salvation and judgment. The power of the word of God cuts the chains and releases a sinner, cutting him away from God eternally.

'He, that being often reproved hardeneth his neck, shall suddenly be destroyed, and that without remedy' (Proverbs 29:1).

There are people who are in covenant with the devil with promises of life. The devil gives them hope and they believe that they will live long, enjoy life and wealth. Such people are deceived because Jesus is the prince of life. Devil and all his agents with their groups cannot give life. When such people enter into covenant with the devil, their neck are hardened by the devil to believe lie. There are many people like that in the church. They don't belong to cults or in covenant with the devil. Satanic agents sends arrows of disobedience. They are in the church, they hear Gods word but they do not have power to obey. They sing, pray in the prayer team, preach as Pastors but has no power to obey. Some of them as preachers, pastors, bishops preach against immorality but they do not have power to say no to immorality. They defy their secretary's right inside their offices. They sleep with their maids and members of their church. This people are under the influence of sin, under the power of sin, so they compromise.

'*Professing themselves to be wise, they became fools*' (Romans 1:22).

'*Therefore thou art inexcusable, O man, whosoever thou art that judgest: for wherein thou judgest another, thou condemnest thyself; for thou that judgest doest the same things... And thinkest thou this, O man, that judgest them which do such things, and doest the same, that thou shalt escape the judgment of God?*' (Romans 2:1, 3).

Jesus Christ is a righteous judge and will not spare you if you commit the sin you preach against. There are people who depend on God's grace to commit sin. The word of God is saying; your judgment will take you unaware, sudden and without announcement. It means, you will not have the chance to repent, confess and be forgiven. It will come without remedy, second chance for you to repent. You cannot deceive God, instead you will end up deceiving yourself. One of the characters of Christ is judgment without remedy. Your life is inviting Christ to display such character each time you compromise in sin. God out of His mercy as Prince of life, Savior is warning you against compromise. If you refuse to repent, confess, forsake and live right, He will judge you. His judgment unto death has no appeal because His judgment is final. You need to be reminded that the same sword that cut you from sin at salvation, delivered you from problems, healed you or made you general overseer, bishop, etc.; can as well cut you off if you decides to remain unrepentant and compromise. God loves you and does not want you to perish or suffer eternally. By the time this letter arrived Pergamos, many members were guilty of compromise. The word of God which is the two edged sword was ready for judgment but as usual, the Prince of life presented life to them first. He was ready to save the repentant first before judgment. Likewise, God is ready presenting life to you and if you repent, you will be saved. The word of God is quick to save anyone who is ready to accept life from the Prince of life. The word of God which is the two edged sword is also quick to judge the unrepentant. It is powerful enough to separate you from any power holding you down in sin, sickness and death. The two edged sword is more powerful than all your problems put together and can quickly deliver you from destruction. It is sharp enough to take you away from any curse, household wickedness, destructions and death. The letter was sent to the believers in Pergamos to assure them that the two edged sword is quick and that deliverance is possible.

'And after three days and an half the Spirit of life from God entered into them, and they stood upon their feet; and great fear fell upon them which saw them. And they heard a great voice from heaven saying unto them, Come up hither. And they ascended up to heaven in a cloud; and their enemies beheld them. And the same hour was there a great earthquake, and the tenth part of the city fell, and in the earthquake were slain of men seven thousand: and the remnant were affrighted, and gave glory to the God of heaven. The second woe is past; and, behold, the third woe cometh quickly. And the seventh angel sounded; and there were great voices in heaven, saying, The kingdoms of this world are become the kingdoms of our Lord, and of his Christ; and he shall reign forever and ever' (<u>Revelation 11:11-15</u>).

'Therefore, it shall come to pass, when the Egyptians shall see thee, that they shall say, This is his wife: and they will kill me, but they will save thee alive' (<u>Genesis 12:12</u>).

'For the word of God is quick, and powerful, and sharper than any twoedged sword, piercing even to the dividing asunder of soul and spirit, and of the joints and marrow, and is a discerner of the thoughts and intents of the heart' (<u>Hebrews 4:12</u>).

No matter the judgment the devil has pronounced upon you, the two edged sword speaking to you from Christ's mouth is quick in action to set you free. You may be the worst compromiser, sinner or wicked person on earth, His two edged sword is quicker than all the evil powers against you. If your business, marriage, academic or health is under arrest, before they destroy you, God's word is quicker in action. If they are planning to condemn you or they have condemned you, your deliverance is quicker than them. You may be in the mouth of your enemy, the word of God is closer and quicker to deliver you. At the time the letter came to the church in Pergamos, many of them have compromised. You may have compromised and told lies, committed murder, entered into cult, sacrificed your life to Satan. Whatever you have done, no matter how bad, you can be delivered. No matter how your church has backslidden, compromised and denied Christ, you can be delivered. No matter your covenant with the devil and abomination you have committed, you can be saved and delivered. Your destiny, glory and star may have been buried, swallowed by any witch or wizard, they can be delivered. The word you are reading now, hearing now is closer to you than your problems. The word you are reading now is quicker in action, more powerful than all your problems and enemies put together. It can cut you off from pains, suffering, barrenness, hardship, poverty and all the attack and is sharper than any power binding you to Satan. It can enter, pierce into the dark room of the devil, enter into any evil altar and hell fire, and take you away without negotiating with your captor. The church in Pergamos was privileged to receive this two edged sword. A sword that can enter anywhere and deliver her captives. A sword that is quickest in action, deliverance and in providing freedom. Two edged sword that is more powerful than all the sickness in and outside hospitals, and outside every home, offices and all places. The sword that is sharper in action than every problem, enemy, Satan and his agents. A sword in Christ's mouth that can divide evil group, satanic kingdom, pierce into heaven and hell without restriction to deliver those who need deliverance. If your problem is inside hell fire, He can pierce into hell. If it is coming from heaven, it can pierce into heaven. If it is from the grave, evil altar, your family or inside your soul, it can enter into them ever before your enemy begin to think against you. If your problem is spiritually, it can pierce into spiritual realm and deliver her captives. This is the two edged sword that Christ put into His mouth when He came to Pergamos. This is the same sword that you are hearing His voice now

'And he had in his right hand seven stars: and out of his mouth went a sharp twoedged sword: and his countenance was as the sun shineth in his strength' (Revelation 1:16).

As He is talking to you now, He has in His right hand, seven Stars. If your star or destiny is in trouble, you are before the Star of all stars. His two edged sword is ready to take action against your enemies, problems and hardships. Christ is ready with every strength to set you free. Don't allow Him to go without asking Him to deliver you. No problem or enemy can stand His countenance that is shining before them as the sun in his full strength. Today is your day of deliverance, freedom and liberty. That day in Pergamos, Christ was ready for action. Today, as you hear this word, He is ready to take action against all your problems. As their heaven was open that day for all manner of deliverance, so is your heaven opened today. If you cooperate with Him, your deliverance will emerge. The white horse of your deliverance, the true Christ has come for your sake, don't let Him go, ask for deliverance. You may have been deceived by fake white horses, undelivered deliverance ministers. You may have suffered from church to church, minister to minister, today is different. The white horse you see today is the true one, the faithful and true Christ, the righteous one who is ready to make war against your problems. He is ready to judge all your problems, enemies and the devil. His eyes can see every hidden enemy, problem in your life and judge them. His eyes is as a flame of fire and every problem in you must be burnt to ashes. He will judge them, war against them with the two edged sword. The sharp sword in His mouth will not spare any of your problems. If you cooperate with Christ, He will deliver you and keep you out of every trouble. It is your turn to experience total freedom

'And there shall come forth a rod out of the stem of Jesse, and a Branch shall grow out of his roots: And the spirit of the LORD shall rest upon him, the spirit of wisdom and understanding, the spirit of counsel and might, the spirit of knowledge and of the fear of the LORD; And shall make him of quick understanding in the fear of the LORD: and he shall *not judge after the sight of his eyes, neither reprove after the hearing of his ears: But with righteousness shall he judge the poor, and reprove with equity for the meek of the earth: and he shall smite the earth with the rod of his mouth, and with the breath of his lips shall he slay the wicked' (Isaiah 11:1-4).*

If your deliverance comes from the Stem of Jesse, no power can stop it. This rod of deliverance like in the days of Moses will overcome every magician, witches and wizards against you. If your deliverance comes direct from Christ, Rod out of the Stem of Jesse, you will never come back to bondage. You have suffered enough from the magicians who say they are deliverance Pastors. You need direct deliverance from Christ who has God's Spirit resting upon Him. Christ who is the Spirit of wisdom and understanding will deliver you today. He knows how to do it, He has the Spirit of Counsel and Might, Knowledge and of the Fear of God. Deliverance with anyone or from any minister and church without the above is fake, incomplete and nothing. Christ came to the church in Pergamos with complete deliverance equipment. He will give you quick understanding in the Fear of God before delivering you. Every wickedness in you from the wicked shall be slain without delay.

'And take the helmet of salvation, and the sword of the Spirit, which is the word of God' (Ephesians 6:17).

'So being affectionately desirous of you, we were willing to have imparted unto you, not the gospel of God only, but also

our own souls, because ye were dear unto us' (1 Thessalonians 2:8).

In other to take part in this deliverance, get direct freedom that comes from Christ, you have to be born again, take the helmet of salvation. Believe the word of God, the sword of the Spirit. If you cooperate with Christ and His word, no enemy or problem will be spared. He will locate and judge every wickedness against you and consume them with the Spirit of His mouth. This is the message that Christ brought to the church in Pergamos. It is disappointing that some people will have this opportunity and fail to respond positively. Today, Christ has come to you as the Prince of life, Savior and Judge. He comes to you having every instrument of deliverance and weapons to deliver and destroy your problems. He comes to you as a Savior of the world, Savior of your soul and body from every satanic attack. Today, He comes to you as God, with His swords which is quick in action, powerful than the most powerful and sharper in operation than all your problems. In His mouth, He came with the two edged sword to speak death unto your problems and to speak life to your body, soul and spirit. He comes to you to enter where no doctor, drugs and surgical instrument has never entered. He want to deliver you, set you free and give you eternal life.

PERGAMOS: THE OFFICIAL CAPITAL OF ASIA MINOR

When Christ sent the letter to Pergamos, He was adequately prepared to deliver them from whatever bondage they entered. He knows the city very well and was well equipped with two edged sword to fight every power behind their problem. No matter where you find yourself or the problem you are going through, Christ knows them better than you,

'And to the angel of the church in Pergamos write; These things saith he which hath the sharp sword with two edges; I know thy works, and where thou dwellest, even where Satan's seat is: and thou holdest fast my name, and hast not denied my faith, even in those days wherein Antipas was my faithful martyr, who was slain among you, where Satan dwelleth' (Revelation 2:12-13).

Pergamos was the official capital of the province of Asia and the seat of imperial authority. One of the prominent symbols on the coinage of Pergamos was serpent.

'Now the serpent was more subtil than any beast of the field which the LORD God had made. And he said unto the

woman, Yea, hath God said, Ye shall not eat of every tree of the garden? And the woman said unto the serpent, We may eat of the fruit of the trees of the garden' (Genesis 3:1-2).

'Notwithstanding I have a few things against thee, because thou sufferest that woman Jezebel, which calleth herself a prophetess, to teach and to seduce my servants to commit fornication, and to eat things sacrificed unto idols' (Revelation 2:20).

The spirit of serpent has entered into the lives of many in the church and deceived them. In the church at Pergamos, deceit and subtlety was the order of the day. All manner of insincerity was being displayed by many members of the church, like anger, fierceness, violence, rape, and all manner of aggression were displayed. Their emblem for Asklepios, the god of medicine, whom they worshipped there was serpent. Pergamos was fortunate to receive one of the letters of the seven churches. Pergamos was the center of four Pagan cults (Zeus, Athena, Dionyus, and Ecclepius) and the seat of the blasphemous Emperor worship. Zeus cult is a powerful god, the king of gods and husband of Herain, Greek, and Mythology compared to Jupiter. Members of this cult are very destructive and some of them came into the church and penetrated into some leaders. Athena is a Greek goddess of wisdom compared to Minerva, while Dionyus is in charge of the ancient Greek festival observances, held in seasonal cycles, in honor of Dionyus, and with dramatic performances. It is also a powerful cult of worship of Dionyus. The other cult is Ecclepius, which bothers on the doctrine relating to the church, or the study of church architecture and adornment. It is the teaching of excessive attachment to ecclesiastical forms and practices. The teachings and lifestyles of these four cult members affected the church in Pergamos. Many of them compromised, that was why Christ spoke of Pergamos as the place where Satan's seat is, and were Satan dwells.

COMMENDATION FOR LONG-SUFFERING

Despite satanic presence, his abode and his seat of power in Pergamos, Christ praised some believers there for their steadfast endurance (Revelation 2:13; 1 Thessalonians 5:21). The presence of the four cult altars, and evil influence of cult members, some brethren especially the church leadership held fast the name of Christ. They refused to bow to serpentine worship of the Emperor. The church held fast Christ's name and refused to bow to satanic pressures. They stood for Christ, kept under His authority, and held His word, seeking only to worship and glorify His name. They did not deny His name, authority, power and word, even in difficult times. They hold fast that which is good and remained firm, and faithful in the darkest spot on earth, where Satan reigns and rules in every space

'And make straight paths for your feet, lest that which is lame be turned out of the way; but let it rather be healed. Follow peace with all men, and holiness, without which no man shall see the Lord' (Hebrews 4:13-14).

They were denied of their rights, benefits and entitlements, yet they determined not to bow down to the devil. Their faith in Christ was challenged and threatened, but they stood their ground and refused to worship the devil. They hold fast their profession of faith without wavering, they believed in Christ's deliverance, even to the point of death. They had multiple needs, great challenges, and impossibilities, but they trusted in Christ's words. Cult members attacked them, challenged their God, and insulted them, but they refused to join cult

'That ye come not among these nations, these that remain among you; neither make mention of the name of their gods, nor cause to swear by them, neither serve them, nor bow yourselves unto them: But cleave unto the LORD your God, as ye have done unto this day' (Joshua 23:7-8).

Some of them died with their problems, but the living ones refused to seek for solution from the cult, they refused and rejected deliverances from the four cults groups. In programs, they refused to mention the names of their gods and preferred to mention the name of Christ. They refused to get their healing, wealth, or swear by the name of other gods, except Christ. They served God in hunger, thirst, pains, and refused to accept anything that will tamper with their relationship with Christ

'And that he was seen of Cephas, then of the twelve: After that, he was seen of above five hundred brethren at once; of whom the greater part remain unto this present, but some are fallen asleep. After that, he was seen of James; then of all the apostles. And last of all he was seen of me also, as of one born out of due time' (1 Corinthians 15:5-8).

'Stand fast therefore in the liberty wherewith Christ hath made us free, and be not entangled again with the yoke of bondage' (Galatians 5:1).

They were steadfast, unmovable, always working for God and doing everything to His glory. They believed in Christ, His reward and faithfulness in the fulfillment of His promises, their limits and liberty was only in Christ. Every other liberty outside the limit of God's word was rejected. How to get rich wealth, get married, bear children, operate in anointing, prophecy that is outside God's word was rejected. They were ready to suffer, starve and die under Christ's liberty than in any liberty with sin. They stood on Christ's liberty, His freedom and refuse to entangle with sin. They refused everything that will bring them again, into the yoke of bondage. Any offer, position, empowerment and joy that has sin attached to it were rejected. They were able to define liberty from the devil and the liberty from Christ. In our present day, many believers and ministers have gone astray. They embraced deliverance, positions, promotions, and empowerments from the cults around us. They step out from Christ's liberty and entangle themselves again with the yoke of bondage because of power and fake deliverances

'Women received their dead raised to life again: and others were tortured, not accepting deliverance; that they might obtain a better resurrection: And others had trial of cruel mockings and scourgings, yea, moreover of bonds and

imprisonment: They were stoned, they were sawn asunder, were tempted, were slain with the sword: they wandered about in sheepskins and goat skins; being destitute, afflicted, tormented' (Hebrew 11:35-37).

'Only let your conversation be as it becometh the gospel of Christ: that whether I come and see you, or else be absent, I may hear of your affairs, that ye stand fast in one spirit, with one mind striving together for the faith of the gospel' (Philippians 1:27).

In Pergamos, some of them were arrested, tortured and promised a lot of blessings if they deny Christ but they refused. Anything you gain, get, achieve outside Christ is useless. Any deliverance that makes you to deny Christ, compromise your faith is false liberty. The church in Pergamos was tried, mocked, put into troubles but they refused to deny Christ. Any promise, conversation that subtract Christ in the church at Pergamos was rejected. They remained steadfast, with one spirit, one mind and strove together to the end

'Be sober, be vigilant; because your adversary the devil, as a roaring lion, walketh about, seeking whom he may devour: Whom resist stedfast in the faith, knowing that the same afflictions are accomplished in your brethren that are in the world' (1 Peter 5:8-9).

They were sober, vigilant and confronted every adversary that tried to influence them against Christ. They resisted the devil, his agents under afflictions and refused to compromise in cult's worships. They refused to follow the errors to avoid a fall from being steadfast in serving God. They believed in the ability of God for their deliverance but in other hand, they made up their mind not to bow down to any idol even without deliverance. Their faithfulness to God was not based on what they will get. They were ready to die pleasing God under any circumstance Acts

'And ye shall be hated of all men for my name's sake: but he that endureth to the end shall be saved' (Matthew 10:22).

They were ready to obey God's word, hear God's word than any other command from anywhere. They made up their mind to go through any suffering, to be hated for the sake of Christ. The believers in Pergamos, in the center of Satan's city had to hold fast to pure worship, pure doctrine and pure Christian life. They prayed for God's grace, received it and remained courageous and uncompromised, fearless and steadfast to the day they received the letter from Christ.

PROBLEM OF FALSE DOCTRINE AND EVIL ASSOCIATION

Despite their faith in Christ, their steadfastness for Christ and contention against the four cults in Pergamos, Christ found out some things wrong in the lives of some members. There were two false doctrines, resulting in evil practices, evil association and unequal yoke held by some people in the church at Pergamos

> 'But I have a few things against thee, because thou hast there them that hold the doctrine of Balaam, who taught Balac to cast a stumblingblock before the children of Israel, to eat things sacrificed unto idols, and to commit fornication. So hast thou also them that hold the doctrine of the Nicolaitans, which thing I hate' (Revelation 2:14-15).

Some held the corrupting doctrine of Balaam, teaching believers to marry unbelievers and eat from sacrifices to idols. The doctrine of Balaam came after Balaam failed to curse the children of Israel. He was invited to curse the children of Israel by king Balak of the Moabites. In the process, they built seven altars into three times but all their enchantment against Jacob failed. In the twenty one altars, they tried divinations but could not succeed

'And when he came to him, behold, he stood by his burnt offering, and the princes of Moab with him. And Balak said unto him, What hath the LORD spoken?' (Numbers 23:17).

'He hath not beheld iniquity in Jacob, neither hath he seen perverseness in Israel: the LORD his God is with him, and the shout of a king is among them' (Numbers 23:21).

'Surely, there is no enchantment against Jacob, neither is there any divination against Israel: according to this time it shall be said of Jacob and of Israel, What hath God wrought!' (Numbers 23:23).

In their enchantment and divination, they discovered that there was no iniquity and perverseness in the camp of Israel. Because of the absence of iniquity and perverseness, the curses could not work. All their enchantments and divinations failed. Anywhere they tried to penetrate the camp of God's people with a curse, righteousness and unity with God blocked the curses. The presence of God was everywhere in the camp and was filled with testimonies of God's greatness and divine presence from every side. In frustration, Balaam advised Balak to use the wayward daughters of Moab to seduce the children of Israel to commit immorality in the camp to remove God's presence and unity among them will be affected. Balaam's counsel was that with sin of immorality, there will be iniquity and perverseness. With iniquity in the camp, God's presence will be withdrawn and disobedience to leadership will take over. There will be disobedience to the shout of the king and the leader's preaching will be despised. That is the beginning of the doctrine of Balaam

It became a way of life, a doctrine that was later accepted, allowed and taught in many churches. It became a way of life in many churches where ladies are allowed to sleep with men before marriage. In some churches today, pastors, ministers, workers and members practice ungodly friendship. Everyone has boyfriends or girlfriends and it is accepted as a way of life. Once someone propose to a lady, they start living like husband and wife. Men, women, married and singles are licensed to commit immorality. Worldly dressings, careless visitations, carnal imitations, sinful practices and all manner of sinful familiarities, foolish talks, and worldly practices are allowed and approved. Pastors, parents receive gifts of money, material things from members and daughters without knowing how they get the money. Programs that encourage immorality among the youths are encouraged

'And Israel abode in Shittim, and the people began to commit whoredom with the daughters of Moab. And they called the people unto the sacrifices of their gods: and the people did eat, and bowed down to their gods. And Israel joined himself unto Baal-peor: and the anger of the LORD was kindled against Israel. And the LORD said unto Moses, Take all the heads of the people, and hang them up before the LORD against the sun, that the fierce anger of the LORD may be turned away from Israel. And Moses said unto the judges of Israel, Slay ye everyone his men that were joined

unto Baal-peor. And, behold, one of the children of Israel came and brought unto his brethren a Midianitish woman in the sight of Moses, and in the sight of all the congregation of the children of Israel, who were weeping before the door of the tabernacle of the congregation.... And those that died in the plague were twenty and four thousand' (Numbers 25:1-6, 9).

After the counsel from Balaam, Balak dressed the daughters of Moab and released them to seduce the children of Israel in the camp. While the children of Israel were camping in Shittim, praising God and thanking him, they saw beautiful girls walking around them. It was the daughters of Moab in their seductive attires. There are churches where their ladies dress like the daughters of Moab. The church in Pergamos overcame false worship, the influence of four cults in their midst but failed in the doctrine of Balaam. When some of the children of Israel in the camp of Shittim saw these beautiful worldly dressed seductive ladies, they lusted after them. Some dresses can distract true worshippers, godly men and powerful ministers. That was what happened at Shittim camp among the children of Israel. So many girls are married today because of the way they dressed, not because it is God's will. That is why there are many problems today in Christian families. That is why the body of Christ is experiencing many separation and divorce today. Many unbelieving women have entered into the church. Their purpose is to seduce pastors, ministers, workers and members. They marry, separate, divorce to cause problems in the body of Christ. They are agents of the devil, looking for believers to destroy. Many pastors, ministers, believers have spiritually divorced their wives, separated because of such seductive ladies, others have killed their partners through witchcraft or physical poisoned to marry their idols.

If God allows every married person to go ahead and divorce today, more than eighty percent of marriages will be ended. When the beautiful daughters of Moab entered into the camp of the children of God in Shittim, the youths and some married men lost their control. Their praise-worship was defiled, polluted and contaminated. Some preachers and interpreters lost their focus and lusted after the daughters of Moab. After the service, power changed hands, phone numbers, contact addresses were changed, appointments in hotels and private places increased. True love in relationships and marriages died completely and lusts replaced them. Within few hours, immorality multiplied and God saw it. Believers fellowship reduced in number and excuses multiplied. The worships, preaching and other godly activities were polluted. There was whoredom and immorality with the daughters of Moab. The preaching of Moses, the king, leaders of God's people on salvation, relationship with God, holiness and God's true power began to irritate the sinful members. God withdraw from the camp.

The daughters of Moab invited them to attend the church, fellowships of compromising preachers, preachers who condone the doctrine of Balaam, worldly dressing and immoral lifestyles. The attendants of churches of occult houses established by the cults in the city increased numerically. They called them unto the sacrifices of their gods and ate and bowed down to their gods. They joined their cults and God's anger was kindled against them. They abandoned the righteousness preaching of Moses and went to ministers who got their powers from evil altars and priests. Their problems multiplied, their hard work culture died and everything about them began to experience problems. All they hear is sow seed, give big offering, no matter how you get the money, you will be blessed. In the process, twenty-four thousands of them died mysteriously. From that day, it became a doctrine that many churches accepted. God hates the doctrine of Balaam and any way of life that makes believers to stumble in faith

'And they warred against the Midianites, as the LORD commanded Moses; and they slew all the males' (Numbers 31:7).

'And Moses, and Eleazar the priest, and all the princes of the congregation, went forth to meet them without the camp. And Moses was wroth with the officers of the host, with the captains over thousands, and captains over hundreds, which came from the battle. And Moses said unto them, Have ye saved all the women alive? Behold, these caused the children of Israel, through the counsel of Balaam, to commit trespass against the LORD in the matter of Peor, and there was a plague among the congregation of the LORD. Now therefore kill every male among the little ones, and kill every woman that hath known man by lying with him' (Numbers 31:13-17).

To show God's hatred for that doctrine in the church or anywhere today, God rewarded the victims with death. He commanded Moses to kill all the males that were involved. All the kings, church leaders, everyone that was involved were killed. All the male and females were judged, condemned unto death. Ministers, churches members who encourage and ignore people with the doctrine are playing with eternity. Jesus Christ who is the Prince of life, the author of salvation can also judge, kill those that practice the doctrine of Balaam

'Thou shalt not follow a multitude to do evil; neither shalt thou speak in a cause to decline after many to wrest judgment' (Exodus 23:2)

'Take heed to thyself, lest thou make a covenant with the inhabitants of the land whither thou goest, lest it be for a snare in the midst of thee' (Exodus 34:12)

'And Jehu the son of Hanani the seer went out to meet him, and said to king Jehoshaphat, Shouldest thou help the ungodly, and love them that hate the LORD? Therefore is wrath upon thee from before the LORD' (2 Chronicles 19:2)

There are many modes of dressings, make ups that God ignored and allowed before but when they became idols, an object of worship, He frowned at them. In many churches today, certain ornaments in the body are becoming idols. It is becoming a show of parade which made them to despise the poor people in their midst. Some hairstyles, fingernails, jewelries and dressing have become objects of worship. I am not against or for any class of dressing or make up but you need to watch your heart. Idolatry is when you put anything before God and it may be external or internal. Believers should not imitate the world system

> 'Blessed is the man that walketh not in the counsel of the ungodly, nor standeth in the way of sinners, nor sitteth in the seat of the scornful' (_Psalms 1:1_).
>
> 'Enter not into the path of the wicked, and go not in the way of evil men' (_Proverbs 4:14_).

Believers must not allow things of the world to influence them or the ungodly to move them out of their place in life. The devil through his deceived agents is spreading the doctrine of Balaam in many churches today. When his agents brought this doctrine in the church at Ephesus, the brethren rejected it

> 'I know thy works, and thy labour, and thy patience, and how thou canst not bear them which are evil: and thou hast tried them which say they are apostles, and are not, and hast found them liars: And hast borne, and hast patience, and for my name's sake hast labored, and hast not fainted' (_Revelation 2:2-3_).

'But this thou hast, that thou hatest the deeds of the Nicolaitans, which I also hate' (Revelation 2:6).

The church in Ephesus hated the deeds of the Nicolaitanes but the Pergamos church embraced it and Christ wrote to warn them of the consequences

In Pergamos, some believers held the corrupting doctrine of Balaam and the heresy of Nicolaitanes. Clement of Alexandria who lived at the time Nicolaitanes practiced their deeds, said they abandoned themselves to pleasure, like goats, leading a life of self-indulgence, immorality, and loose living. They replaced liberty with license and perverted grace. They came to Pergamos with these two doctrines, the doctrine of Balaam and the Nicolaitanes and they accepted them. Though Christ praised them for their steadfastness endurance and victory over cults in their city, they were defeated with the problems of false doctrines. It is good to take this warning because you may be fervent, vibrant and militant against cults but compromise in false doctrines. What was Christ's response, contrition or command to church in Pergamos?

PENITENCE COMMANDED

Christ the Prince of life, Savior and Judge wrote to the church in Pergamos and commanded them to repent. He was ready to save the penitent ones among them. He did not present judgment first to them, rather He presented salvation. His will for them, to you and to us all is not to condemn but convince, convict and convert them. There is no heart too hard that cannot be surrendered to Christ, give up sin, or sin committed that cannot be pardoned. If you can believe the gospel, come to Christ's light, you will be saved and not judged. You can only be fought by Christ and condemned if you believe not, love darkness, love the deed of evil, hate light, refuse to come to light or neglect the great offer of salvation.

'Repent; or else I will come unto thee quickly, and will fight against them with the sword of my mouth' (Revelation 2:16).

'How shall we escape, if we neglect so great salvation; which at the first began to be spoken by the Lord, and was confirmed unto us by them that heard him' (Hebrews 2:3).

Christ gave the church at Pergamos the offer to repent, confess and forsake their sin of compromise for false doctrines. It is when you despise the offer, neglect, believe not, love darkness, and hate the light offered to you that Christ will fight you, condemn you and allow you to suffer eternally

'If my people, which are called by my name, shall humble themselves, and pray, and seek my face, and turn from their wicked ways; then will I hear from heaven, and will forgive their sin, and will heal their land' (2 Chronicles 7:14).

'But if the wicked will turn from all his sins that he hath committed, and keep all my statutes, and do that which is lawful and right, he shall surely live, he shall not die' (Ezekiel 18:21).

'Cast away from you all your transgressions, whereby ye have transgressed; and make you a new heart and a new spirit: for why will ye die, O house of Israel?' (Ezekiel 18:31).

Christ wrote to the church at Pergamos that if they humble themselves, repent of practicing false doctrine, pray, seek His face, turn away from every wicked practice, He will give them true life and they will be saved and not be judged. Everything the devil through false doctrines, evil association has stolen from them will be restored, if they repent. Their marriages, relationships and business will be healed. There are things God expects from you, every family or church to do so that deliverance will come. Deliverance does not come only through prayer. You need to humble yourself, believe in Christ, come to the light, walk in the light, pray, seek God and believe that your prayers are answered. No matter how wicked a wicked person is, if he turns from all his sins, keep God's command, start living right, he will receive divine mercy, life, salvation and not judgment. That was what Christ told the brethren in Pergamos. If a sinner cast away his transgressions, pray for a new heart, he will be saved, no matter how unsafe he was

'And as they did eat, Jesus took bread, and blessed, and brake it, and gave to them, and said, Take, eat: this is my body' (*Mark 14:22*).

'And the son said unto him, Father, I have sinned against heaven, and in thy sight, and am no more worthy to be called thy son' (Luke 15:21).

Christ know all things, your weakness and short comings. He knew that the church in Pergamos will fall to false doctrines and evil association. He made provision for their repentance and put it in writing. Even Peter, His closest disciple denied Him thrice, but He gave him another chance. No matter how sinful, wicked and abominable you are, if you repent and confess your sins and forsake them, Christ will give you a new life, save you and set you free. The consequence of every sin you have ever committed, all your wickedness can be removed and forgotten forever and ever

'Remember therefore from whence thou art fallen, and repent, and do the first works; or else I will come unto thee

quickly, and will remove thy candlestick out of his place, except thou repent'(Revelation 2:5).

'As many as I love, I rebuke and chasten: be zealous therefore, and repent. Behold, I stand at the door, and knock: if any man hear my voice, and open the door, I will come in to him, and will sup with him, and he with me' (Revelation 3:19-20).

God's command to the sinful members of the church in Pergamos is repent. They are to repent in going after the world, false doctrine and evil associations. Check your life, find where you need to repent, confess and forsake now. Remember where you have fallen in faith, offended God and repent, do the first works, the right thing and your judgment will be reversed. It is out of love that Christ has for the church, the brethren in Pergamos that made Him to send this letter to them first. He sent the letter to warn them, rebuke them, chastise them and command them to repent. You have the same opportunity to examine yourself, be zealous and repent of all your sins and forsake them. As Christ stood at the door of the church in Pergamos, knocking with a letter in His hands, so He is doing today in every church. Every believer, leader, member of the church today must examine themselves, repent and examine the life that Christ gives. Today, if you repent, open the door of your church, your heart to Christ, He will come in and solve all your problems, He will deliver you from compromise, sin and their consequences. Without repentance, judgment will fall on all disobedience. If you wed yourself with the world, God will judge you, and fight against you until you repent or perish.

PROMISE FROM THE PRINCE OF LIFE

OBEDIENCE TO GOD'S WORD, remaining faithful, being unmovable in serving the Lord to the end is not in vain. There is a reward attached to every service or obedience to God's word. Christ assured the brethren in Pergamos that if they obey, repent from going after the world, abandon the false doctrine of Balaam and the deeds of Nicolaitanes, they will be rewarded. He assured them of a promise for being pure in heart and life.

> 'He that hath an ear, let him hear what the Spirit saith unto the churches; To him that overcometh will I give to eat of the hidden manna, and will give him a white stone, and in the stone a new name written, which no man knoweth saving he that receiveth it' (Revelation 2:17).
>
> 'Blessed are the pure in heart: for they shall see God' (Matthew 5:8).

Having an ear is only profitable when the hearer hears what the Spirit of God says. Ears become unprofitable to its owner and the hearer when it does not hear what God's Spirit says. Today, God's Spirit is still speaking to the church but few are hearing. The few that heard but refused to obey what they heard will be punished also. From Genesis to Revelation, the Spirit of God has been talking. Adam and Eve had ears when they were told not to eat a particular fruit in the garden but instead of hearing and obeying, they heard the devil and obeyed his voice. The wife of Lot heard what the Spirit of God said but she despised what she heard and looked behind. Joseph's brother heard what God's Spirit said concerning love but they ignored it and hated their brother, envied him and conspired against him, sold him and told lies to their Father. Christ wrote to the church at Pergamos and at the closing remark of the letter,

He assured the hearers of a promise if they obey. Reading this letter is okay, hearing what the Spirit of God is telling the church is good, but only the obedient will receive the promise. Pharaoh heard all that the Spirit of God had said concerning letting the children of Israel out of his bondage. He has ears to hear but lacked the power to obey. He heard all the warning for disobedience from Moses but he conspired and afflicted the children of Israel. He said who is God? He refused to let Israel go and he died for his disobedience. Nadab and Abihu were ordained priests, sons of Aaron, and were instructed on how to handle God's work. They heard what God's Spirit said, but instead, they offered strange fire and died right inside the altar

'And Nadab and Abihu, the sons of Aaron, took either of them his censer, and put fire therein, and put incense thereon, and offered strange fire before the LORD, which he commanded them not. And there went out fire from the LORD, and devoured them, and they died before the LORD' (Leviticus 10:1-2).

Today, as a minister, no matter your rank, you must hear and obey what the Spirit of God is saying to the church. Pergamos church has come and gone, but the Spirit of God is still talking to you and to the church of every nation. Korah, Dathan, Abiram and all the renowned men of Moses days heard all that the Spirit of God said through Moses but they choose to disobey, they choose their reward, as the earth opened her mouth and swallowed them alive. Balaam heard God's word and His plans and God's promises to Israel but because of the love of money, he went ahead to curse God's children. Achan heard all the instruction from Joshua concerning the accused things but because of covetous spirit in him, he took the accused things, the Babylonian garments and he was stoned to death. Samson was advised against strange women, women of contradicting faith in God but he went by sight, preferred a harlot, lusted after Delilah and lost his power and two eyes in a battle. The sons of Eli were ordained priests, well instructed about priesthood in the best theological school of their time but they choose not to know God, broke God's commandment, fornicated in God's house and died in a battle. Saul the first king of Israel was anointed by Samuel, instructed by Samuel, prayed for by Samuel but chose to disobey God's word. He got angry easily and attempted to kill David and sought for the service of a witch with a familiar spirit and died by committing suicide. Ahitophel was empowered by God with wisdom, he knew how to give good counsel but he compromised and associated with a sinner, counseled Absalom who stole the heart of God's people. He died after his last wicked counsel was rejected by committing suicide.

Solomon was a chosen king, preferred above his brethren, counseled by David but he left good counsel and loved many strange women, shifted his heart, turned from God, built idol, made affinity with pharaoh and married his daughter. The man of God, the young prophet clearly heard God's word before he went to Bethel. But he listened to the old backslidden prophet, went back to his vomit, ate, drank against God's word and died in shame. Ahab was preached to by Elijah, he heard all the prophecies of Elijah, but turned away his ears from hearing what the Spirit said. He did evil above Jeroboam, married Jezebel, worshipped Baal, built houses for Baal's prophets, made groves and rebuilt Jericho wall. He entered into covenant with Ben-hadad, God's enemy, took Naboths vineyard and hate Micah, God's true prophet. Gehazi heard his master when he rejected the gift from Naaman but went after him, told lies and received the gifts. What will I say for time will fail me to talk about the people, nations that disobeyed Gods word through prophet Isaiah, Jeremiah, Daniel, etc? What of the Pharisees, the Sadducees, the young rich men, Judas Iscariot, the thief in the left hand of Jesus at the cross, the scribes, the chief priests, the passersby in the cross, Herod, Pilate, the parents of a man born blind and the multitudes who all heard the direct preaching of Christ but laughed Him to scorn, and refused to obey His words. Remember Christ's promise, His assurance to the obedient believers, hearers in Pergamos. The promise for the pure in heart and life. They were promised two things, the hidden manner, and the white stone

'Follow peace with all men, and holiness, without which no man shall see the Lord' (<u>Hebrew 12:14</u>).

'Blessed are they that do his commandments, that they may have right to the tree of life, and may enter in through the gates into the city' (<u>Revelation 22:14</u>).

Overcomers are peaceful people, people of holiness and pure heart. They are hearers who hear God's word and obey. They keep God's commandment and try to please God at all cost even unto death.

CHAPTER FIVE

FOURTH LETTER

THE TRUE PROPHET

Revelation 2:18-29

Christ, the true prophet of God with His eyes open to see even in the dark sent letters to the seven churches in Asia. In those letters, He commended, warns, rebukes, encourages and extends His promises to all who have ears to hear in every church. Right now, we are studying His (letter) message to the church in Thyatira. In this church, Christ opened His eyes and saw a false prophetess who was permitted to teach and wrongly influence the members.

'And unto the angel of the church in Thyatira write; These things saith the Son of God, who hath his eyes like unto a flame of fire, and his feet are like fine brass' (Revelation 2:18).

For a very long time, this false prophetess with the spirit of Jezebel has deceived many in the church without being noticed. She occupied a very prominent position, a seat in the church, with recognition by the church leadership. Her teachings influence many members to adopt her sinful lifestyle. All other teachers and leaders in Thyatira came under her influence. They were all possessed by the spirit of Jezebel.

'And he shall send Jesus Christ, which before was preached unto you: Whom the heaven must receive until the times of restitution of all things, which God hath spoken by the mouth of all his holy prophets since the world began. For Moses truly said unto the fathers, A prophet shall the Lord your God raise up unto you of your brethren, like unto me; him shall ye hear in all things whatsoever he shall say unto you. And it shall come to pass, that every soul, which will not hear that prophet, shall be destroyed from among the people' (Acts 3:20-23).

Christ with His eyes like a flame of fire saw this false prophetess in her full deceit and destructive ministry. With a letter, He walked into the church with His feet, like a brass. As the true, steadfast and faithful prophet from God, He confronted this fake and false prophetess like no one had done before. If you are in a church where you rule and reign without challenge wrongly, Christ is here with a warning letter.

If your sinful lifestyle has influenced others in the church or the community and yet, none has preached to you, open your ears. If you promote sin, evil lifestyle anywhere and yet, none has rebuked you, warned you, Christ, the true and faithful Prophet cannot be afraid of you. If you have a place, position, authority in any ministry, church and influence others to sin, you have a warning letter from Christ. If you are a leader, an overseer and you live a life of sin, influence others without rebukes, a warning letter, Christ the steadfast, faithful Prophet is writing you today. All leaders, people with a seat, position of any kind in all the churches on earth are being warned with a letter from Christ today.

If you are a leader who influence people under you wrongly, be warned. You may not have access to offering money but your way of life, teachings influence people under you to tamper with God's money, be warned. If your teachings, prophecy or style of leadership promotes sexual immorality, separation, divorce or any kind of sin, this may be your last or only warning letter. The truth is that this rebuke or warning letter is coming from the faithful Prophet of God. If you have despised other rebukes and warnings and got away with them, this one is coming from heaven, the faithful Prophet of God. This preaching is coming from Christ, this one which all prophets spoke about since the world began. The Prophet that Moses saw and told the fathers of Israel that God will raise as a Prophet. The Prophet that Moses commanded us to hear in all things.

No matter your position in any church, you must hear Him. You may be the founder of your church, you must hear Him. You may be the general overseer, you must hear Him. You may be an arch bishop, an apostle, the leader of other leaders, you must hear Him. You may run your church, your branch as a personal property, business, you must hear Him now. You may have lived this way all your life, influencing people wrongly, this time, you must hear Him. You may have mismanaged the ministry, people under you, lived like Jezebel, you must hear Christ now. Whether you read this letter or not, every disobedient person will be judged. For those who are privileged to read this letter, obedience is demanded you may have despised other letters and go free, you may have despise other letters and go free, you must not despise this one. The author is Christ the one that Moses told even the fathers of Israel to obey. No matter how old you are, your place in the church, you are not older than the fathers of Israel

This is a Prophet recognized by God, from heaven, approved by the Almighty, spoken about by Moses, respected by the fathers of Israel. He is the true and faithful Prophet, raised by God.

'For mine eyes are upon all their ways: they are not hid from my face, neither is their iniquity hid from mine eyes' (Jeremiah 16:17).

'Can any hide himself in secret places that I shall not see him? saith the LORD. Do not I fill heaven and earth? saith the LORD' (Jeremiah 23:24).

You may have all the nine gift of the Holy Spirit, healing, miracle, prophecy etc., you must hear this Prophet. You may be intelligent, highly respected and reverenced, you must hear this Prophet. You may have dominated everyone in the church because of your gift, you cannot dominate this Prophet. If you do not hear this Prophet, obey this

Prophet, you will be destroyed from among the people. Whatever you have achieved in the church, no matter your contributions, you must hear this Prophet. Moses called the fathers of Israel to hear Him in all things, whatsoever He shall say. Christ is that Prophet, the faithful and steadfast Prophet from God, raised by God and commissioned to write to me and you and we must hear. Every way you followed in the past, present and will follow in the future, His eyes are seeing you clearer.

None of your activities, prophecies, secrets is hidden from His eyes, He sees all. There is no iniquity that can be hidden from His eyes. All your past are exposed before Him. Every activity going on earth, in heaven, in the church, everywhere is exposed before His eyes. Ministers, prophets, pastors and members activities are exposed to His eyes. You, I have no option than to come before Him in repentance and ask for forgiveness.

'He revealeth the deep and secret things: he knoweth what is in the darkness, and the light dwelleth with him' (Daniel 2:22).

'And it shall come to pass at that time, that I will search Jerusalem with candles, and punish the men that are settled on their lees: that say in their heart, The LORD will not do good, neither will he do evil' (Zephaniah 1:12).

It is foolishness to think or believe that you have a secret before God. He knows all our activities, thoughts and imaginations ever before we were born. This letter is telling us to acknowledge our sins and repent. Our most darkness, deep secrets, things are exposed before the eyes of this faithful Prophet. He is light and light live with Him and can never be separated from Him. The eyes of Christ are the source of all seeing eyes and the candles of the world put together.

> 'And needed not that any should testify of man: for he knew what was in man' (John 2:25).

> 'Neither is there any creature that is not manifest in his sight: but all things are naked and opened unto the eyes of him with whom we have to do' (Hebrews 4:13)

This Prophet has no need to search, ask question, investigate, or enquire of anyone's activity before He knows it. He knows all men, their pasts, present and the end of every end from the beginning.

> 'His head and his hairs were white like wool, as white as snow; and his eyes were as a flame of fire; And his feet like unto fine brass, as if they burned in a furnace; and his voice as the sound of many waters' (Revelation 1:14-15).

Christ has eyes like flame of fire and can see all things without obstruction. What He is saying is that He is still in charge of every church. No church belonged to anyone, any overseer, any pastor or prophetess. His letter to the church is, I am still in-charge, in control and will judge anyone of any rank who refuse to obey. If you are gifted to heal, deliver or prophesy, Christ is saying, you need to know that all gifts come from Christ. He sees all things, all people, and all believers in all churches clearly. His vision is not blocked, cannot be blocked or dimmed by human ignorance or wisdom. He cannot compromise His standard and His judgment is without fear or favor. In the Day of Judgment, you cannot stop Him; block His feet, which are like fine brass. He will overthrow any opposition and tread under His feet all enemies of truth and righteousness.

'Then cometh the end, when he shall have delivered up the kingdom to God, even the Father; when he shall have put down all rule and all authority and power. For he must reign, till he hath put all enemies under his feet. The last enemy that shall be destroyed is death. For he hath put all things under his feet. But when he saith, all things are put under him, it is manifest that he is excepted, which did put all things under him' (1 Corinthians 15:24-27).

Whatever you are doing in the church, outside the church, it will end one day. Christ's letter is saying to you, do everything according to the rule. Your time will end one day, your service will come to an end one day. You cannot occupy the seat, your position forever. You will be asked to give an account for your stewardship. The head of the church will call you for an account and nothing is hidden from His eyes. You may be the boss, the master and an overseer. Jesus is saying; I am the Big Boss, the master of all masters and the highest overseer. He is going to ask you for an account and you must not hide anything that day. He sees all, knows all and can get to anywhere with His feet of brass and remind you even of those things you have forgotten. He will put all rules, including your position to an end one day. Every authority, power, including the one you are using now will surrender to Christ. As a pastor, leaders, prophet, an overseer, try to do everything according to the rule. Christ, the faithful Prophet is the only one His reign will last forever. Do not lead others; rule others as if you are the last boss, overseer. If you choose to rule, reign, do things your own way, just know that one day Christ will put all enemies under His feet. Even death shall be destroyed that day how much less all the false prophets.

'For the Father judgeth no man, but hath committed all judgment unto the Son' (John 5:22).

'And many believed on him there' (Acts 10:42).

If there is anyone to submit your royalty to, it must be Christ. Do not allow the fear of backslidden godfathers, leaders and your flesh to put you at enmity with Christ. If you have to say no to anyone, let it not be to Christ. Every judgment is committed to Christ by God, not to your earthly leader. Christ has the final say, not your overseer. So do everything to the glory of God and not to please man. If you die trying to do the right thing, to obey Christ, those who kill you cannot judge you anymore. The last judge you will meet after death is Christ, so do everything to please Him unto death. Preach the way Christ asks you to preach, testify as He ordained you and don't divert church fund to please any godfathers. Do not compromise; re-model your ministry to suit anyone except Christ. Fight the good fight, fulfill your ministry and please Christ to the end.

'Because he hath appointed a day, in the which he will judge the world in righteousness by that man whom he hath ordained; whereof he hath given assurance unto all men, in that he hath raised him from the dead' (Acts 17:31).

'In the day when God shall judge the secrets of men by Jesus Christ according to my gospel' (Romans 2:16).

'But why dost thou judge thy brother? Or why dost thou set at nought thy brother? For we shall all stand before the judgment seat of Christ' (Romans 14:10).

Christ's will not judge you according to your faithfulness to man but to His word. You must read His letter to the churches and do everything possible even unto death to obey His commands. He will not be bribed in the Day of Judgment and none can influence Him against you.

'Therefore seeing we have this ministry, as we have received mercy, we faint not' (2 Timothy 4:1).

If your leader is fighting you because you are obeying God's word, Christ will reward you on the Day of Judgment. Every secret plot against you for obeying Christ will be exposed on the Day of Judgment. If you pray now, in this program, the judgment can start now and you will be vindicated. No matter what it will cost you, don't ever disobey God's word, fight to the end.

PROGRESS IN THYATIRA CHURCH

As I study the seven letters to seven churches in Asia, I discover to my shock and surprise that there is no place that one cannot achieve greatness. I also discovered that every church is a mixture of good and evil, wheat and tares, true and false. For some brethren to make progress in the church in Thyatira is remarkable.

'And unto the angel of the church in Thyatira write; These things saith the Son of God, who hath his eyes like unto a flame of fire, and his feet are like fine brass' (Revelation 2:18).

'Saying, I am Alpha and Omega, the first and the last: and, What thou seest, write in a book, and send it unto the seven churches which are in Asia; unto Ephesus, and unto Smyrna, and unto Pergamos, and unto Thyatira, and unto Sardis, and unto Philadelphia, and unto Laodicea' (Revelation 1:11).

Thyatira was an interesting little place 30 miles from Sadis and Pergamos. The city was built for one purpose – to act as an interceptor to any army approaching Pergamos, the capital of Asia Minor. It delayed any troops long enough to allow Pergamos to get ready to fight them. It was a military garrison to protect Pergamos. It also developed commercial significance as it became center of dying clothes, which were sold in various parts of the known world.

> 'And a certain woman named Lydia, a seller of purple, of the city of Thyatira, which worshipped God, heard us: whose heart the Lord opened, that she attended unto the things which were spoken of Paul' (Acts 16:14).

Lydia was fortunate to worship God in the city of Thyatira and was prospered by God in purple business. The major problem of every Christian is to discover their place in life and face what God has called them to do in righteousness. Ministers who complain of lack of progress in their city must pray to discover their place in life, their relationship with God and their assignment. Believers in Ephesus with the present of Diana goddess made progress. In Pergamos, a place described as the seat of Satan, the devil bowed to the true believers who lived in that city. They made progress and served God in truth and in spirit. The best progress any child of God will make in any place is to serve God. Many believers in many cities are not serving God, yet they complain of lack of progress. There is no church too good or too bad to stop any believer's progress if he stands for righteousness to the end. Many believers cannot challenge the seat of Satan where they live. The believers in the city of Thyatira were under the attack of a filthy prophetess. Some committed members overcame the spirit of Jezebel in the woman and lived holy.

'I know thy works, and charity, and service, and faith, and thy patience, and thy works; and the last to be more than the first' (Revelation 2:19).

They were able to discern and know the right people to be helped. They were charitable, serviceable and faithful to the end. It was not easy for them at the initial stage but they were patient enough to wait for God's time. The problem with many believers in many churches is lack of patient. They are carnal and do not have the fruits of the spirit.

'But the fruit of the Spirit is love, joy, peace, longsuffering, gentleness, goodness, faith, Meekness, temperance: against such there is no law' (Galatians 5:22-23).

When you love God, His word and work, you can face any battle. The love of God will compel you to stay where God assigned you to stay and face the enemy. The joy of victory ahead of you will motivate you to keep fighting, praying and believing God for victory to the end. You will not abandon your duty post, assignment in the church because of a filthy prophetess or an agent of the devil. You will keep seeing victory, joy that wait for you at the end of the tunnel without fainting. Unless you did not discover, find out your place in that church or city. But if you do and face your divine call, assignment and love for God, you will surely make progress. Progress brings joy and joy from God leads to peace, settlement and establishment in life.

To make progress anywhere you are divinely located, you have to be steadfast, committed to your divine given assignment unto the end. To achieve this, you must be born again and manifest the fruits of long suffering which will lead you to greatness in any place. With the above, you will make progress, live a gentle life, do well and faithfully serve God with what He has blessed you with. Once you are settled where God has called you, meek spirit and temperance will be your definition. Many people need to prayerfully cast out the spirit of vagabond and fugitive from their life. You need to get your place in life, know your divine call, assignment in life and manfully fight residential powers. You need to discover the filthy prophetess, enemy of defilement and destruction and fight them in other to make progress.

'The righteous also shall hold on his way, and he that hath clean hands shall be stronger and stronger' (Job 17:9).

'Behold, O God our shield, and look upon the face of thine anointed' (Psalm 84:9).

When you get born again, discover your place in life, divine assignment, the next battle is to establish permanent relationship with God and His children. This will deliver you from evil association and from any agent of the devil. With that, you will discover and reject the evil influence of filthy prophetess, filthy people and all satanic agents. The victorious believers in Thyatira maintained good life, lived righteous, kept God's way, refused to be influenced and polluted by the filthy prophetess in their midst. They made progress in their ministry, business and God blessed the works of their hands.

To some of them, their progress was delayed, stopped and attacked but they never compromised. They kept their relationship with God, lived holy, kept their hands clean and served God. It was not easy for them to worship God in a place where the filthy prophetess ruled but they persisted to the end. One day, they gained strength and victory was achieved and they made progress. They received deliverance, achieved greatness and lived for Christ in the city of Thyatira. My Father in the Lord, Pastor W. F KUMUYI, said; Holiness is not a big deal but the real deal. And holiness is never an excuse for poverty. You can be richly holy. Our great and humbly father, E. A. ADEBOYE said; Humility is not stupidity or mediocrity. You can live in humility, purity and prosper at the same time. My Oga, father in the Lord; DR. D. K. OLUKOYA said; In the school of destiny discovery, recovery and fulfilment, everyone is a fighter, consciously or unconsciously. You have to fight against something if you must be anything in life. Bishop DAVID O. OYEDEPO said; Faith is a risk you must continue to take if you must continue to be a burden to none and a lift to others. The strength of the Thyatira came from God, prophecy came from God and deliverance came from God. Today, the question everywhere is, can your pastor prophecy, see vision, heal and deliver me? No one is interested on the source of prophecy, power and anointing. Once someone who does not know God's word, respect God's word or live holy can prophecy, you will see cloud and great multitude. There are very few today who seek for God's word or righteous pastors who have clean hands. In other to keep members, get members, many pastors have defiled their hands. Every Pastor, Minister wants to be a prophet or prophetess. Very few ministers are still holding to the way of the Lord. Many have left the way of righteous living, they have polluted their hands and co-operated with the devil for fake power. They have left Zion, Christ, forsake the truth for filthy prophecies from the dark kingdom. Many pastors, church founders, bishops and overseers need deliverance from the spirit of Jezebel and her mother, the woman that sits upon many waters.

'And I saw the woman drunken with the blood of the saints, and with the blood of the martyrs of Jesus: and when I saw her, I wondered with great admiration' (Revelation 17:6).

'And he saith unto me, The waters which thou sawest, where the whore sitteth, are peoples, and multitudes, and nations, and tongues' (Revelation 17:15).

This is the woman that distributes fake powers and the spirit of Jezebel. Many ministers are guilty and they need deliverance with the members of their congregation. This woman, the mother of Jezebel has made many ministers, prophets and prophetess, walking corps. She has killed them, drank their blood while they are alive. She gives ministers power to sit upon their ministry, health, business, and finances and upon their members. Many ministers have sold their lives, ministries and worse, their members to this evil woman. That is why many people in the church are suffering, dying in their problems without help.

> 'And he saith unto me, The waters which thou sawest, where the whore sitteth, are peoples, and multitudes, and nations, and tongues' (_Revelation 17:15_).

She is sitting upon their destinies, marriages, health, and greatness one by one and in their multitudes. Many great ministers, their ministries and members need deliverance but they do not know how to go about it. Their source of power is fake, filthy and demonic. They are in trouble with their members and under the yoke of filthy prophets, prophetess and ministers.

> 'And Jabez called on the God of Israel, saying, Oh that thou wouldest bless me indeed, and enlarge my coast, and that thine hand might be with me, and that thou wouldest keep me from evil, that it may not grieve me! And God granted him that which he requested' (_1 Chronicles 4:10_).

> 'But the path of the just is as the shining light, that shineth more and more unto the perfect day' (Proverbs 4:18).

'Enlarge the place of thy tent, and let them stretch forth the curtains of thine habitations: spare not, lengthen thy cords, and strengthen thy stakes' (Isaiah 54:2).

The family of Jabez changed his pattern of family prayer through Jabez. You need to change your pattern of prayer. You need to seek for deliverance from ministers who still keep clean hands. You need to call upon Christ direct. He is the true and faithful Prophet with power to deliver you from every captivity. This letter is an avenue to link you up to your true Prophet, the great deliverer and the coming king. This is time to leave darkness and come to the true light which is Christ. You can ask for personal deliverance now and get it. You have the opportunity to get your deliverance direct from Christ right away. No matter how much you have backslidden or gone away from the true light, you can come back. Christ is the true Prophet and you can receive prophecy direct from Him now. There is no place you are that Christ cannot reach at you and deliver you if you ask for deliverance.

You can still make progress in ministry, in business, in marriage and in any area of your life. Some of this prophets and prophetess you run to are not real or better than you. They are agents of the devil and under deceit to deceive others. Jesus is the only true and faithful Prophet. Some of the prophetess and prophets are in covenant with the devil and the woman that sits upon many waters. They can prophecy, tell you stories but cannot cast out the spirit behind your problems. They can tell you the truth but they lack power to deliver you out of trouble. Let me tell you what some of them do. They are in covenant with the devil to sanction your problems for some times. They do not cast out demons or solve problems. Others with the power of fake prophecy like the woman in our text called Jezebel can see without solution. Others, which is the third group transfer demons or problems from leg to hand, head to business, father to mother or anywhere. Some of these prophets, prophetess and ministers you run after operate with the under listed triple "S". They

(1)   Sanction problems for a season

(2)   Seeing problems, defining it without bringing permanent solution and

(3)   Sending your problem from one area of your life to another. They are worse than the prophetess in Revelation, our text called Jezebel, a filthy prophetess. In deliverance school, college and university, we called them prophets, prophetess and ministers with triple "S", they are deceivers. They operate with the counterfeit of Satan.

'For such are false apostles, deceitful workers, transforming themselves into the apostles of Christ. And no marvel; for Satan himself is transformed into an angel of light. Therefore it is no great thing if his ministers also be transformed as the ministers of righteousness; whose end shall be according to their works' (2 Corinthians 11:13-15).

Some of them can prophesy but their lives are filled with greed, pride, anger, immorality, covetousness, financial irresponsibility, jealousy, unfaithfulness, cultic and all manner of fleshy lusts. They are swindlers, carnal without any robe of righteousness. Some believers in the church at Thyatira overcame her in the church and Christ congratulated them. They were commended for their significant spiritual progress over the filthy prophetess. They overcame her by bearing the fruits of the spirit. They had true love for Christ in service, faith, patient and endurance to the end. Though, the church in Thyatira lacked sound doctrine by tolerating or allowing the woman to function but some members overcame her evil teaching and way of life.

FILTHY PROPHETESS

There are many false prophetess and prophets that has overcome many pastors, church leaders and their members. They used witchcraft powers to bewitch everyone in the church and they now operate without challenge. Those who dare challenge them are under attack and as a result, they silence everyone and operate without opposition.

'Notwithstanding I have a few things against thee, because thou sufferest that woman Jezebel, which calleth herself a prophetess, to teach and to seduce my servants to commit fornication, and to eat things sacrificed unto idols. And I gave her space to repent of her fornication; and she repented not' (Revelation 2:20-21).

The one Jesus discovered in the church in Thyatira was allowed to operate like Jezebel. She took over the teaching department in the church with seductive spirits. Many great servants of God in that church was seduced and influenced to commit fornication and to eat things sacrificed to idols. She had the opportunity to repent many times but like a pig, she was so domineering that even some true servants of God were victims to fornications. She was a specialist in putting people under the yoke of sin for compulsory evil actions. She is called Jezebel because she had the ability to force, influence or compel people to commit fornication. She can get whatever she wants by any means at all cost. Like the Jezebel of the Old Testament, wrote a letter, sealed it with the senior pastor's name and signature to get anything she wants. Such people with Jezebel's spirit have entered into many pastors, God's servant and use their names to get whatever they wanted. The elders of the church are under their command because she has seduced some with gifts, sexual immorality or witchcraft powers.

'And Jezebel his wife said unto him, Dost thou now govern the kingdom of Israel? arise, and eat bread, and let thine heart be merry: I will give thee the vineyard of Naboth the Jezreelite. So she wrote letters in Ahab's name, and sealed them with his seal, and sent the letters unto the elders and to the nobles that were in his city, dwelling with Naboth. And she wrote in the letters, saying, Proclaim a fast, and set Naboth on high among the people: And set two men, sons of Belial, before him, to bear witness against him, saying, Thou didst blaspheme God and the king. And then carry him out, and stone him, that he may die' (1 Kings 21:7-10).

They can organize any program, get information and prophesy accurately without solving any problem. She can set uncompromising victims up, raise alarm and influence people to tell lies against people. Many false prophets, prophetess is in charge of many congregations today. Any branch pastors who refuse to bow to her seductive demand are flamed up, sacked, removed from their branch to the village to go and prove their ministry. She has killed people's ministries, marriages and starved many God's servant to death with arrows of witchcrafts. Many have lost their ministries and faith in Christ as a result of their constant attacks. Jezebel spirits has taken over many ministries. Some of them has killed overseer's wives or forced them to divorce to marry them. They now control everything in the church through the general overseer and turned God's church into private company. Many women's womb are closed, others are suffering from marital delays and hostilities in marriage.

They spread immoral spirits, sinful lifestyles and weakness in the congregations. They empower their agents to seduce God's servants, members of the church to make sure that they are unfit for heaven. They fire arrows of problems into people's life, prophesy to them and cause them to come under their control. The actions of filthy prophets have taken many pastors away from God. They operate in diverse ways and many of them are unnoticed. Some are visibly operating, why many operate through ministers in charge. They speak through pastors, leaders in authority and such class of filthy prophets and prophetess are difficult to dictate. Some of them who succeeded in getting married to pastors, leaders are in control through such leaders. Their voices and actions are delivered through anyone they possess.

'And it came to pass, as if it had been a light thing for him to walk in the sins of Jeroboam the son of Nebat, that he took to wife Jezebel the daughter of Ethbaal king of the Zidonians, and went and served Baal, and worshipped him. And he

reared up an altar for Baal in the house of Baal, which he had built in Samaria. And Ahab made a grove; and Ahab did more to provoke the LORD God of Israel to anger than all the kings of Israel that were before him' (*1 Kings 16:31-33*).

Ministers who are possessed with the spirit of Jezebel are wicked but they become more wicked when they are bewitched to marry women or men with such spirits. Once they possess a pastor, an overseer, the one in charge of any group, their first aim is to destroy the good people around their victim. They flame up righteous people, frustrate holiness teachers and replace them with their agents. They frustrate good ministers within and without the ministry. If you insist on remaining, they will place you under attacks, problems until they kill your ministry and force you to compromise. If you go out, they will still attack you to make sure you do not succeed in ministry, business or anything you try to do. Jezebel spirit's target is against God's true servants and their anointing.

'For it was so, when Jezebel cut off the prophets of the LORD, that Obadiah took an hundred prophets, and hid them by fifty in a cave, and fed them with bread and water' (*1 Kings 18:4*).

'Now therefore send, and gather to me all Israel unto mount Carmel, and the prophets of Baal four hundred and fifty, and

the prophets of the groves four hundred, which eat at Jezebel's table' (1 Kings 18:19).

They fight true ministers; replace them with false prophets, teachers and evil leaders. They can hire false prophets, gather all their old members, especially women who no longer give birth, place them on salary to pray and fast against God's servants who left their ministry. Jezebel can pay false prophets and prophetess to do any evil against God's ministers. If you are at her good book, you are sure of big branch in the ministry, good benefits and promotions without hard work. She can place a royal Jezebel spirit filled minister and empower them to use offering money without accounting to it. You can eat at her table all through your life on earth. If you leave a Jezebel controlled ministry, you must prepare for war. They vow to see that nobody leave their ministry and prosper.

'And she wrote in the letters, saying, Proclaim a fast, and set Naboth on high among the people' (1Kings 21:9).

'They proclaimed a fast, and set Naboth on high among the people' (1Kings 21:12).

When you are under the attacks of the spirit of Jezebel, you have to be strong. Their first aim is to dominate you, overcome you and use you to achieve their aim inside the ministry. To achieve that, she has to seduce you to commit fornication with her. The fornication here means to seduce you and bring you under the control of many, few or at least a sinful lifestyle you can never say no to all your life. By so doing, they will make you a candidate of hell fire, a child of devil and kill your relationship with God forever. The second is to use you to bring other people in the ministry, around you under such sins and reduce you to a seducer through such sinful practices. They can allow you to be an unconscious member of their group but they can never allow you to live without such sinful lifestyle. After that, every good thing in your life will begin to have problems. Your ministry, job, business, marriage and all that gives you joy will begin to die gradually. Because you are under the yoke of sin, the more you pray for deliverance, the more your attack increases. If you seek for their help, deliverance, they will give you deliverance prayer to pray but you can never get deliverance with the yoke of sin in your life.

If you seek for deliverance in another ministry, they will hire their conscious members who eat or benefit at their table to pray and fast against you. If you dare leave their ministry, they will release demons from their kingdom to bear witness against you, influence people to hate you and reject you everywhere you go. They will cause you to make terrible and painful unimaginable mistakes that will cause good people and good things to avoid you. They will set you up; possess weak people to attack you and to frustrate your efforts in life. They will spiritually block your way and physically invoke enemies against you anywhere you go. People will hate you without knowing why they hate you. They will increase your battles, disorganize you and force you to seek help in wrong places. If you have anyone in your family, church or office with the spirit of Jezebel, you need Christ and Him alone to deliver you. Ministers who left them go through a lot of battle and if really they have anything against you, you will suffer terribly. That is why most ministers like that enter into cultism to survive under double bondage.

'And Ahab told Jezebel all that Elijah had done, and withal how he had slain all the prophets with the sword. Then Jezebel sent a messenger unto Elijah, saying, So let the gods do to me, and more also, if I make not thy life as the life of one of them by tomorrow about this time' (1 Kings 19:1-2).

If you want to leave such ministry, I advise you, leave with clear mind. Do not remove any of their things, property or money. Have a clear conscience and make sure you are guided by God. Jezebel spirit has messengers, agents in every office all over the world. They have powerful network to locate anyone under them before in a movement of time. They are under oath with gods to kill, destroy any enemy. They can use the weapons of hunger, thirst, lack and the whole creature to fight. Even the righteous victim with clear mind is not spared. You must have knowledge, wisdom and be an expert to use the weapons of warfare to survive their attacks. The message of jezebel alone to Elijah was very destructive and scarring. Elijah who fought many battles and won ran away from ordinary voice of witchcraft. They can release fear from the throne of fear to attack even righteous servants of God how much less a sinner. Elijah ran away and abandoned his servants, forgot his responsibility. He preferred death instead of life and prayed for it. Many children of God are being pursued today by the voice of witchcraft. Their arrows of sickness, poverty, lack, hunger and good things of this world are worse than death. Many people who commit suicide are as a result of witchcraft voice pursuing them. Jezebel spirit can attack a man, deny you of your rights, benefits, entitlement and chase many helpers and good witness far away from your reach. When she was attacking Naboth for his vineyard, all his relations, friends and helpers abandoned him to suffer and die alone. That is why some people will have rich relations, prosperous friends and yet suffer without helpers. That is why some people lose every good thing they have in the battle field of life and yet die.

If you are under the judgment of the spirit of Jezebel, all your helpers will not be around in the time of your trouble. Those who are around will not understand why they are not assisting you. The problem from the spirit of Jezebel will take your vineyard and still kill you in shame. You may have children, wife, brothers, friends but they will not give you job or render any help to you. They will watch you to suffer under pains, wants and sorrow unto death. People will know the truth but they will not talk. They will have the opportunity to save you, help you and make you great but they will not act. Everybody will hate you, fight you and those who will not join them will watch you suffer and die. This is the spirit that possessed the woman in the church at Thyatira and every minister bowed. They allowed her to teach prophecy and seduce God's servants.

She overcame the ministers, seduced them and took over the pulpit. The senior pastor, the overseer and all the workers abandoned the bible study, teaching ministry for her to decide who teach. The woman took over everything and seduced God's servants. There are many churches like that everywhere today. No more teaching, evangelism. Everything is deliverance, prayer, prophesy and entertainment with no emphasis on the need of repentance and the word of God.

TERRIBLE PUNISHMENT

The filthy prophetess in the church in Thyatira overpowered the ministers and members with her false teaching of deceit. She seduced the members of the church with her powerful witchcraft and the spirit of Jezebel. She spread immorality and mislead many with idolatrous worship. Christ sent a letter and confronted her with terrible and fierce judgment.

> 'Behold, I will cast her into a bed, and them that commit adultery with her into great tribulation, except they repent of their deeds. And I will kill her children with death; and all the churches shall know that I am he which searcheth the reins and hearts: and I will give unto every one of you according to your works' (Revelations 2:22-23).

God hates sin and brings judgment against unrepentant sinners. Every backslider and sinners in the church will be rewarded. Ministers and members who practice and teach evil in any place will not go free. All whose lifestyle promotes sin and influence people to rebel against God's word will be judged and punished fiercely by God. No unrepentant sinner will go free unpunished. Sinners and their followers will be cast into the bed of affliction. In times of their trouble, no one will be able to help or deliver them. Their children and all their supporters will suffer at the same time. In the past, the spirit of Jezebel hates and kills believers without negotiation but today, she negotiates. This is the spirit that demanded the head of John the Baptist and got it. This is the spirit that stoned Stephen unto death. This spirit fought and killed all the Apostles except John. This spirit entered into kings, leaders to persecute the church. By the time Christ wrote the seven letters to the seven churches, this spirit was in all the seven churches persecuting them.

The Emperor of Rome Domitian was used as human weapon by the spirit of Jezebel. At that time, the spirit entered into the Emperor to arrest John. John was the only Apostle of Christ remaining alive. Others were persecuted and killed. She put John through all forms of suffering and troubled him to deny Christ but he remained steadfast. He was very old at that time but he refused to surrender to all the negotiations presented to him by Jezebel. Finally, they decided to boil him alive in a drum of boiling oil. In the midst of the boiled oil, he escaped alive miraculously. They took him to exile and dropped him in the midst of wild animals in an isle of Patmos. While he was there alone in the midst of unfriendly breeze, winds, abandoned to suffer and die, he saw a vision. Christ appeared to him in His full priesthood, full glory, authority, wisdom, purity, victory and omniscience. The Lord Jesus manifested in the isle of Patmos to visit His abandoned servant in a princely and true prophetic office. If you are going through any persecution, attacks from the spirit of Jezebel, your time for deliverance has come. Christ knows where you are abandoned, what you are going through now, your time of deliverance has come. The Christ that John ate and dined together came to save him. Christ did not come like He used to come when John knew Him.

'And when I saw him, I fell at his feet as dead. And he laid his right hand upon me, saying unto me, Fear not; I am the first and the last: I am he that liveth, and was dead; and, behold, I am alive for evermore, Amen; and have the keys of hell and of death' (Revelation 1:17-18).

He came with total wisdom, complete purity and with a piercing, penetrating insight and full knowledge. Jesus appeared to John with full glory and triumph over all powers, enemies and all problems. He came in the greatness of His power and final authority, in His great beauty and brilliance to judge the spirit of Jezebel in the church. At that point of His appearance, John and all his righteousness could not stand the righteousness, the glory, the majesty and the authority that accompanied Christ from heaven. He could not stand the light, so he fell down at Christ's feet as dead. Christ touched him with His right hand and introduced Himself as the first and the last. Jezebel with all her problems upon you is not the first and the last. They do not have the final say over your life. If she has killed your health, ministry, marriage, business or everything in you and buried them. Christ has the keys of where she locked you, the keys of every graveyard, hell and death. Your deliverance will take place. Christ banished every fear and told John to stop fearing. In the midst of an Island, a lonely place, void of human existence, Christ visited him. Where you are now is better than where John was, yet Christ visited him and delivered him. Even if you were swallowed by a witch, a wizard or death, they will vomit you today, right now. Christ appeared to John with a new ministry, a commission.

'Write the things which thou hast seen, and the things which are, and the things which shall be hereafter; The mystery of the seven stars which thou sawest in my right hand, and the seven golden candlesticks. The seven stars are the angels of the seven churches: and the seven candlesticks which thou sawest are the seven churches' (Revelation 1:19-20).

He gave him a pen, a writing material to write. He started writing under divine command. From today, your dream life will change; you will see vision and a new commission from Christ. In obedience to the commission, John wrote chapter one of sixteen and God opened his eyes wider again. What did God, Christ show him? What did he see, who was that and why did Christ show him?

'And there came one of the seven angels which had the seven vials, and talked with me, saying unto me, Come hither; I will shew unto thee the judgment of the great whore that sitteth upon many waters' (Revelation 17:1).

He was invited by one of the seven angels to a throne, the headquarters of Jezebel, a great whore, a great prostitute that sitteth upon many waters. He was told that this woman will be judged. She will not go free of all her persecutions, attacks and abominations against the church. John was brought to the day the woman, the Jezebel that used the emperor against him will be judged. John was alive, fit, strong and in faith the day his enemy will be judged and his full deliverance from every trouble. You have seen so many problems, faced all manner of attack in life and have really suffered. But thank God you are alive today to see the judgment of the personality in charge of all your troubles. John was called to see the judgment of the woman in charge of all his suffering in life, problems in the churches. This woman, all her unrepentant agents and children will be judged, they will face fierce and terrible judgment.

> 'Behold, I will cast her into a bed, and them that commit
> adultery with her into great tribulation, except they repent
> of their deeds. And I will kill her children with death; and all
> the churches shall know that I am he which searcheth the
> reins and hearts: and I will give unto every one of you
> according to your works' (_Revelation 2:22-23_).

John was clearly shown how this woman deceived the kings of the earth, used Emperor Domitian and other great leaders against the church. He was shown how this filthy prophetess committed fornication and made the inhabitants of the earth to be drunk with her fornication. John saw this filthy woman in the wilderness, decked with gold, every good thing with a golden cup in her hand that was filled with abominations. John was shown and told that this woman is in charge of all the abomination going on everywhere on earth. John saw how this filthy woman killed many saints and drank their blood and sits upon the destinies of many living saints in the church. After seeing all this things, the woman tried to negotiate with John. She began to present all the good things she normally used to deceive the saints. She presented purple, all manner of good things, gold, precious stones, pearls to John. And surprisingly, John dropped his writing pen, materials and began to admire her with great admiration. John was bewitched, manipulated and deceived but the angel intervened.

'And I saw the woman drunken with the blood of the saints, and with the blood of the martyrs of Jesus: and when I saw her, I wondered with great admiration. And the angel said unto me, Wherefore didst thou marvel? I will tell thee the mystery of the woman, and of the beast that carrieth her, which hath the seven heads and ten horns' (Revelation 17:6-7).

'And he saith unto me, The waters which thou sawest, where the whore sitteth, are peoples, and multitudes, and nations, and tongues' (Revelation 17:15).

The angel pulled John backward and cautioned him against any covenant, negotiation with the woman. The angel told John that the water which he saw in Revelation chapter seventeen verses one is not ordinary water but human beings. She came to the church in Thyatira and sat upon their destinies, marriages, health, glory, business and every good thing. This is the last woman to fight before any believer will get a true blessing. This is the woman that suffered many believers, cornered them and entered into covenant with them to deny them of real deliverance. This is the woman that negotiated with God's true ministers and caused them to backslide.

This is the woman that deceived many ministers and empowers them with fake power to perform lying wonders, fake miracles. This is the woman that is suffering many believers, ministers and church members. This is the woman that many ministers receive power from, wealth from, healing from, children from and all temporary blessings. If you have any enemy, this woman is your worst enemy. If there is any enemy to avoid, this is number one. If you have to fight war or kill, this is the personality to destroy first. If you want true anointing, power, wealth, peace, joy and any blessings, fight this woman first. The bible called her MYSTERY, BABYLON THE GREAT, THE MOTHER OF HARLOTS AND THE MOTHER OF ABOMINATIONS OF THE EARTH.

'And upon her forehead was a name written, MYSTERY, BABYLON THE GREAT, THE MOTHER OF HARLOTS AND ABOMINATIONS OF THE EARTH' (Revelation 17:5).

6

My joy is that God has decided to judge her in your life, in the church and in Thyatira but you must not admire her. You must not envy believers, cult people and ministers she had empowered. You must remain faithful to the end until your deliverance comes. These modern days, she has changed her style of operation in the churches. She can empower her deceived ministers, general overseers to do good, preach sound doctrines, pretend to preach about heaven but when you go close to them, you will find devil's nature in them. She empowers some of his agents, ministers to draw crowd but majority will never make heaven.

Their deliverance is fake, temporary with triple "S". In some of her minister's ministries, they fight each other, kill one another, fear one another and avoid one another. She put her agents in salary by prospering them with good things in life like she did in the tome of Elijah but one day, her 400 false prophets died without help. Their salvation message, holiness, preaching and deliverances are not complete, holy, pure and godly. Let me tell you one way to identify the ministry she controls. They do certain things to the extreme and pretend to be persons they are not. Secondly, once you belong to their ministry, you get testimony, miracle, healing, deliverance or solution you are looking for. Thereafter, you lose those things and all the good things you came with. You will then be at their mercy and if you want to leave, they will attack you.

DELIVERANCE FROM JEZEBEL

Whenever we talk about deliverance from Jezebel, we mean the water spirit, the woman that sits upon the waters and the queen of heaven

'And there came one of the seven angels which had the seven vials, and talked with me, saying unto me, Come hither; I will shew unto thee the judgment of the great whore that sitteth upon many waters: With whom the kings of the earth have committed fornication, and the inhabitants of the earth have been made drunk with the wine of her fornication. So he carried me away in the spirit into the wilderness: and I saw a woman sit upon a scarlet coloured beast, full of names of blasphemy, having seven heads and ten horns. And the woman was arrayed in purple and scarlet colour, and decked with gold and precious stones and pearls, having a golden cup in her hand full of abominations and filthiness of her fornication: And upon her forehead was a name written, MYSTERY, BABYLON THE GREAT, THE MOTHER OF HARLOTS AND ABOMINATIONS OF THE EARTH. And I saw the woman drunken with the blood of the saints, and with the blood of the martyrs of Jesus: and when I saw her, I wondered with great admiration. And the angel said unto me, Wherefore didst thou marvel? I will tell thee the mystery of the woman, and of the beast that carrieth her, which hath the seven heads and ten horns' (Revelation 17:1-7).

'Then all the men which knew that their wives had burned incense unto other gods, and all the women that stood by, a great multitude, even all the people that dwelt in the land of Egypt, in Pathros, answered Jeremiah, saying, As for the word that thou hast spoken unto us in the name of the LORD, we will not hearken unto thee. But we will certainly do whatsoever thing goeth forth out of our own mouth, to burn incense unto the queen of heaven, and to pour out drink offerings unto her, as we have done, we, and our fathers, our kings, and our princes, in the cities of Judah, and in the streets of Jerusalem: for then had we plenty of victuals, and were well, and saw no evil. But since we left off to burn incense to the queen of heaven, and to pour out drink offerings unto her, we have wanted all things, and have been consumed by the sword and by the famine' (Jeremiah 44:15-18).

Moreover, any deliverance that does not start and affect spiritual part is not recognized by God. That is why many people pray for deliverance but their case get worse. Any deliverance that does not spiritual provokes Jezebel and attracts more attacks from the kingdom of darkness is not complete. If you want real deliverance in life, you have to fight unto death, if need be. If Jezebel, water spirit does not see this decision in you, before and during deliverance, you are likely not going to be delivered. When one takes decision for Christ unto salvation, you are expected to live for Him or die for Him. It is not conditional or with an option, it is a must, no negotiation or compromise.

If the water spirit sees any condition or an option in your decision to follow Christ, she will negotiate. Be ready to live, survive, perish or die serving the Lord without option, no second chance or part two. With this single decision, even if you make mistake, Christ will pardon you and deliver you.

> 'But Peter and John answered and said unto them, Whether it be right in the sight of God to hearken unto you more than unto God, judge ye. For we cannot but speak the things which we have seen and heard' (Acts 4:19-20).
>
> 'And now, behold, I go bound in the spirit unto Jerusalem, not knowing the things that shall befall me there: Save that the Holy Ghost witnesseth in every city, saying that bonds and afflictions abide me. But none of these things move me, neither count I my life dear unto myself, so that I might finish my course with joy, and the ministry, which I have received of the Lord Jesus, to testify the gospel of the grace of God' (Acts 20:22-24).

When you are praying for deliverance, the first thing the powers behind your problem will search for is your level of decision for Christ, how deep it is, the extent you are ready to go with Christ. Remember that at salvation, you gave your life to Christ as an offering. If the power behind your problem know that you are likely going to withdraw back your life, compromise, you are likely not going to get the deliverance, if you do, it is not complete, permanent or from God. Deliverance candidate must first surrender their lives to God without condition. Your deliverance from physical infirmity is not more important than your soul or relationship with Christ, your faith in Him. Deliverance candidate seeking for true deliverance must be ready to fight a good fight of faith, finish their course, keep faith at all cost and earnestly contend to the end, life or dead. The devil, Jezebel and their entire agent know that your faith is a priceless treasure and they are ready to negotiate with you to exchange it with anything in earth.

Nothing must be exchanged with your faith in Christ. In times of distress, trials, perplexity, pressure and all trouble, you must fight to the end, even unto death to keep your relationship with Christ. Paul, other apostles and the Old Testament saints persevered to the end and they never allowed the threats of kings, oppositions, fiery furnace, sickness, late marriage, hunger, shame, suffering, hardship or death to sweep off their faith. They fought to the end, believed their God and held fast their faith in the darkest hour when all the foundations on which men of the world built their hopes were ruthlessly swept away.

'Shadrach, Meshach, and Abed-nego, answered and said to the king, O Nebuchadnezzar, we are not careful to answer thee in this matter. If it be so, our God whom we serve is able to deliver us from the burning fiery furnace, and he will

deliver us out of thine hand, O king. But if not, be it known unto thee, O king, that we will not serve thy gods, nor worship the golden image which thou hast set up' (Daniel 3:16-18).

The disciples were ready to obey God, keep faith than to obey men. They refused to negotiate with the devil and his agents. Paul was ready to go into bondage, die in it rather than negotiate. Nothing on earth moved him and his life was less important to him than his relationship with Christ. His decision was to keep faith, finish his course and fulfil his ministry with joy which he received from Christ. The three Hebrews children who were probably younger than you did not prefer their life above their faith in God. They looked at Nebuchadnezzar to his face and dared him and his gods. As small as they were at that time, they were not afraid of the burning fiery furnace, suffering in fire unto death. They told the king who was surrounded by his security men, the mightiest that were ready to die the worst death than to compromise their faith in God to worship idol. The king commanded his army to bind them. He was full of fury and his visage changed but all this did not move those little boys who knew the value of their relationship with God. He commanded the furnace to be heated seven times more than the normal heat. That was abnormal but abnormal fire met with abnormal children with abnormal faith. Sometimes you need to be abnormal to survive Jezebel. God did not deliver them outside the burning fire. They were delivered inside the fire. You don't need to force God through your prayer how He should deliver the life you handed over to Him at salvation, they no longer belong to you. The problem with many deliverance candidates is too much love and idolatry in their body, physical life. They are afraid to face the enemy that has only power to kill the body. As a result, they hand over their soul but tried to save their body. At the end of their ends, they lose both the body and the soul in hell.

'And fear not them which kill the body, but are not able to kill the soul: but rather fear him which is able to destroy both soul and body in hell' (Matthew 10:28).

Deliverance candidates must do everything possible to preserve their soul. If God can preserve the cups, vessels of gold that Solomon handed over to Him for seventy years, He will preserve your life which is more important than ordinary cups. He judged Belshazzar for drinking with golden vessels dedicated to Him

'Belshazzar, whiles he tasted the wine, commanded to bring the golden and silver vessels which his father Nebuchadnezzar had taken out of the temple which was in Jerusalem; that the king, and his princes, his wives, and his concubines, might drink therein. Then they brought the golden vessels that were taken out of the temple of the house of God, which was at Jerusalem; and the king, and his princes, his wives, and his concubines, drank in them. They

drank wine, and praised the gods of gold, and of silver, of brass, of iron, of wood, and of stone. In the same hour came forth fingers of a man's hand, and wrote over against the candlestick upon the plaister of the wall of the king's palace: and the king saw the part of the hand that wrote' (<u>Daniel 5:2-4</u>).

'Then Daniel answered and said before the king, Let thy gifts be to thyself, and give thy rewards to another; yet I will read the writing unto the king, and make known to him the interpretation. O thou king, the most high God gave Nebuchadnezzar thy father a kingdom, and majesty, and glory, and honor: And for the majesty that he gave him, all people, nations, and languages, trembled and feared before him: whom he would he slew; and whom he would he kept alive; and whom he would he set up; and whom he would he put down. But when his heart was lifted up, and his mind hardened in pride, he was deposed from his kingly throne, and they took his glory from him: And he was driven from the sons of men; and his heart was made like the beasts, and his dwelling was with the wild asses: they fed him with grass like oxen, and his body was wet with the dew of heaven; till he knew that the most high God ruled in the kingdom of men, and that he appointeth over it whomsoever he will. And thou his son, O Belshazzar, hast not humbled thine heart, though thou knewest all this; But hast lifted up thyself against the Lord of heaven; and they have brought the vessels of his house before thee, and thou, and thy lords, thy wives, and

thy concubines, have drunk wine in them; and thou hast praised the gods of silver, and gold, of brass, iron, wood, and stone, which see not, nor hear, nor know: and the God in whose hand thy breath is, and whose are all thy ways, hast thou not glorified: Then was the part of the hand sent from him; and this writing was written. And this is the writing that was written, MENE, MENE, TEKEL, UPHARSIN. This is the interpretation of the thing: MENE; God hath numbered thy kingdom, and finished it. TEKEL; Thou art weighed in the balances, and art found wanting. PERES; Thy kingdom is divided, and given to the Medes and Persians. Then commanded Belshazzar, and they clothed Daniel with scarlet, and put a chain of gold about his neck, and made a proclamation concerning him, that he should be the third ruler in the kingdom. In that night was Belshazzar the king of the Chaldeans slain' (Daniel 5:17-30).

Many deliverance ministries and their ministers are negotiators. They are in covenant with Beelzebub, the queen of heaven and Jezebel. They are not allowed to deliver, cast out devil but to suspend, sanction for a season or transfer. As you go through this program and meet up with Christ's demand for deliverance, you will be delivered. You do not need to run up and down, looking for prayer and deliverance contractors or negotiators. Deliverance can take place now and here. If your life is with God, your soul is with God, and all things are possible with God.

'And Samuel spake unto all the house of Israel, saying, If ye do return unto the LORD with all your hearts, then put away the strange gods and Ashtaroth from among you, and prepare your hearts unto the LORD, and serve him only: and he will deliver you out of the hand of the Philistines. Then the children of Israel did put away Baalim and Ashtaroth, and served the LORD only' (1Samuel 7:3-4).

Stop deceiving yourself and do not let deliverance contractors to keep deceiving you. You can get deliverance from the devil or his agents but they will not profit you at the end of the ends. You need to go back to God now with all your heart. You need to renounce all the gods in your life, put them away, and prepare to serve only God and pray for deliverance. I have personally been oppressed, I saw affliction by the rod of devil's wrath. The devil took me to darkness where there was no light and turned against me all nights and days. My flesh was attacked, my bones broken with evil spirit around me with gall and travail. The devil and his agents had once hedged me about and shut out my payers. But one day, I cried to God, surrendered everything to Him and my deliverance appeared right in front of me. If I can be delivered, your case is not impossible. I used to pray, cry to God, saying, when will I start a day and end it without pains, troubles, shame, disgrace and reproach? But today, the game has changed. God told the fainting people in Thyatira, the few that rejected the doctrine of Jezebel that deliverance is possible.

'But unto you I say, and unto the rest in Thyatira, as many as have not this doctrine, and which have not known the depths of Satan, as they speak; I will put upon you none other burden. But that which ye have already hold fast till I come' (*Revelation 2:24-25*).

He told them to hold fast to the end till He come. If you have compromised, you can now return to God, confess your sins and forsake them and Christ will deliver you, set you free from every problem. If you are in the midst of the conflict with Jezebel, Christ is telling you now, hold fast till I come, don't give up but continue to fight.

'And he that overcometh, and keepeth my works unto the end, to him will I give power over the nations: And he shall rule them with a rod of iron; as the vessels of a potter shall they be broken to shivers: even as I received of my Father. And I will give him the morning star. He that hath an ear, let him hear what the Spirit saith unto the churches' (*Revelation 2:26-29*).

'And he said unto him, Well, thou good servant: because thou hast been faithful in a very little, have thou authority over ten cities' (*Luke 19:17*).

'Do ye not know that the saints shall judge the world? And if the world shall be judged by you, are ye unworthy to judge the smallest matters? Know ye not that we shall judge angels?

How much more things that pertain to this life?' (1 Corinthians 6:2-3).

If you are about to give up, compromise, hold your faith fast, your deliverance is not far. If you keep your faith, overcome in this conflict, you will rule and reign over all your enemies. There is a gift with your name on it from Christ, so hold fast. You are going to receive a star that will launch you into your morning, a place of strength, full of power with undefiled blessings. You must hold fast, wait to the end to receive this star. You need to be faithful, remain faithful to the end. Your angel of deliverance is just by your door, hold fast, your deliverance is hungry to appear and embrace you.

The overcomers are those who keep Christ's works unto the end. They shall reign with Christ at the down of His kingdom.

CHAPTER SIX

FIFTH LETTER

DEATH IN THE CITY CHURCH

Revelation 3:1-6

The church in the city of Sardis was under attack from the spirit of death. Their attacks started in the spirit and many good things in them died without notice, Christ saw it and became sorrowful.

'And unto the angel of the church in Sardis write; These things saith he that hath the seven Spirits of God, and the seven stars; I know thy works, that thou hast a name that thou livest, and art dead. Be watchful, and strengthen the things, which remain, that are ready to die: for I have not found thy works perfect before God' (*Revelation 3:1-2*).

Because of Christ's concern for them, He sent the letter we now read to them. As the bride groom of the church, the Savior and shepherd, His heart was broken when He saw the extent of the spiritual damage. He was concern and sorrowful because His purpose of suffering and death for the church was defeated. He died to raise a strong, militant, lively, vibrant and spiritual church. But here, reverse was the case, they were dead spiritually. His title as the Alpha, Omega, the first and the last was removed and transferred to death. The candlesticks, the light of the church in Sardis was removed and replaced with thick darkness. Their spiritual condition broke the Heart of Christ, brought concern to Him and moved Him to write this letter to the remaining contending members.

The star of that church's branch was arrested by death and their love for Christ was dead. The ministers were only concerned about their personal welfare while the members' life was slaughtered by death. The flock, the lambs, the sheep was feeding the ministers with their physical blessings, tithes, offerings and all manner of seed sowing but they starved them off spiritual food. The condition of the members were dead spiritually, formal, cold, sinful and that caused Christ great sorrow to His heart.

> *'And unto the angel of the church in Sardis write; These things saith he that hath the seven Spirits of God, and the seven stars; I know thy works, that thou hast a name that thou livest, and art dead... Thou hast a few names even in Sardis, which have not defiled their garments; and they shall walk with me in white: for they are worthy' (Revelation 3:1, 4).*

'Saying, I am Alpha and Omega, the first and the last: and, What thou seest, write in a book, and send it unto the seven churches which are in Asia; unto Ephesus, and unto Smyrna, and unto Pergamos, and unto Thyatira, and unto Sardis, and unto Philadelphia, and unto Laodicea' (<u>Revelation 1:11</u>).

Christ entered the church with the Seven Spirits of God and Seven Stars and saw their works. They had a big signpost, a name well known in the city. They have members in every building in the city, every office, and ministry and in market places. The people that matters in the government know them. Their presence is well represented in every major event, programs, songs of praise and deliverance exploit raised alarm in every street in the city but they were dead spiritually before God. Heaven does not recognize all their deliverance services. They were out of coverage area and their cries could not reach God. Their name as a ministry was dead before God and prayers diverted and could not cross the second heaven. Their activities, meeting places, conventions and great deliverance programs were not approved by God.

'And to speak unto the priests who were in the house of the LORD of hosts, and to the prophets, saying, Should I weep in the fifth month, separating myself, as I have done these so many years? Then came the word of the LORD of hosts unto me, saying, Speak unto all the people of the land, and to the

priests, saying, When ye fasted and mourned in the fifth and seventh month, even those seventy years, did ye at all fast unto me, even to me? And when ye did eat, and when ye did drink, did not ye eat for yourselves, and drink for yourselves? Should ye not hear the words which the LORD hath cried by the former prophets, when Jerusalem was inhabited and in prosperity, and the cities thereof round about her, when men inhabited the south and the plain?' (Zechariah 7:3-7).

'Now Joshua was clothed with filthy garments, and stood before the angel. And he answered and spake unto those that stood before him, saying, Take away the filthy garments from him. And unto him he said, Behold, I have caused thine iniquity to pass from thee, and I will clothe thee with change of raiment. And I said, Let them set a fair mitre upon his head. So they set a fair mitre upon his head, and clothed him with garments. And the angel of the LORD stood by. And the angel of the LORD protested unto Joshua, saying, Thus saith the LORD of hosts; If thou wilt walk in my ways, and if thou wilt keep my charge, then thou shalt also judge my house, and shalt also keep my courts, and I will give thee places to walk among these that stand by' (Zechariah 3:3-7).

All their years of weeping, fasting, mourning and struggles in ministry was dead before God. All their great singings were dead before God. The money, talents, evangelistic moves, car dedication, houses and great cathedrals was just a show of pride, they were dead before God. Their prosperities, multiplication of branches from city to city, they only built visible church but could not build them spiritually.

All their activities were dead before Christ. They labored for death and made him the Alpha and Omega, the first and the last of their activities on earth. Most of their leaders were witches, wizards and in cults. They have big names, titles, and they struggle, fight over positions, big branches, kill and destroy destinies among themselves. Some of them were called but was carried away by the things of this world. They entered into competition with devil-empowered godfathers, church council and lost their ministry. They commit adultery, fornication, practice witchcraft, hate one another, manifest anger, envy each other, murder opponents and use church money to enrich themselves. They fight, kill, and tell lies; steal church money to bribe fallen godfathers to get a big branch in the commercial city of Sardis.

THE CITY OF SARDIS

Sardis was located some fifty miles east of Smyrna, on the south side of the fertile valley of the Hermus, just where the river Pactolus issued from the Timolus Mountains. Its extensive fruit orchards, its textile industries, its jewelry factories and its great wealth derived from the gold mined from the sands of the Pactolus River, made it one of the richest and most powerful inland cities of the ancient world. In Sardis, it is said to have been minted the world's first coins and Croesus (kresus), its famous ruler during the 6th century B.C., was so fabulously rich that even since his time men have said, "as rich as Croesus". Sardis was captured by Cyrus in 546 B. C.; and Alexander the great in 334 B.C.; then destroyed by an earthquake in 17 B. C. It was rebuilt by the Romans and converted to Christianity during the first century A. D. and it survived until Jamerlane swept over the country in 1402 and almost completely destroyed the place. Only a small village named sart lies near the site of the ancient city Sardis.

THE UNRIGHTEOUS CHURCH

The lifestyle of the unbelievers in Sardis affected the life of the church members in the city of Sardis. When Paul arrived as a missionary in the city of Athens, he saw sophisticated structures and massive buildings. It was the home of many of the scholars and orators of the ancient age. The education, architecture, pleasures, social development in that developed city did not move or impress him. Rather, his spirit was stirred in him when he saw the city wholly given to idolatry. His spirit saw beyond the superficial because the city was spiritually dead. He went into the market and evangelized among the common people. He entered the synagogues and preached to religious people. He went to mars hill, the highest court in the land and evangelized the specially chosen high-class decision makers. But in Sardis, reverse was the case.

The ministers in Sardis church allowed the worldly lifestyle in the city to control the life of the members. Christ our perfect example gave up everything; position, right, glory, life to reconcile man to God. When He accomplished the mission, He left the world and went to the father in heaven. When He left, He left His body, the church behind to carry out and continue the same mission, to reveal God to man.

The church has a ministry to the redeemed and the lost. We are to witness, worship, testify and teach Christ's life. Believers in the church are people saved and separated from the world. The leaders, bishops or overseers in the church are to protect the members from heretics, false prophets and worldly lifestyles. They are to rebuke sinners and stand for the truth. The members of the church is to live their lives to glorify God, worship Him, learn, evangelize, be faithful at work, office, profitable at home and prayerful at all times.

Through series of divine motivated programs, the church is expected to effectively penetrate into sinners in the community and change their lives. It is the responsibility of the church in the city to reach everyone in the city with the gospel message to show forth the glory of God. The far reaching scope of the mission of the church demand that every believer by all means propagate the gospel message (1 Corinthians 9:19-22). From house to house, in the villages, towns, cities and in countries beyond our borders, make them decide for Christ and live righteous (Romans 15:20-21). Instead of accomplishing this mission, the elders, bishops, ministers and members of the church like today in Sardis brought the world into the church and made it a sinful church. This action affected the church in several ways:

THEY BECAME SPIRITUALLY DEAD

The church in Sardis was carried away by pleasures and the wealth of the city and they sold their birthright. They became spiritually dead and broke the heart of Christ.

'*And unto the angel of the church in Sardis write; These things saith he that hath the seven Spirits of God, and the seven stars; I know thy works, that thou hast a name that thou livest, and art dead*' (*Revelation 3:1*).

'*And you hath he quickened, who were dead in trespasses and sins; Wherein in time past ye walked according to the course of this world, according to the prince of the power of the air, the spirit that now worketh in the children of disobedience: Among whom also we all had our conversation in times past in the lusts of our flesh, fulfilling the desires of the flesh and of the mind; and were by nature the children of wrath, even as others*' (*Ephesians 2:1-3*).

The prince of Sardis, the worldly spirit that ruled the land worked through the leaders and promoted disobedience. They indulged in all manner of lusts to fulfill their fleshly desires among themselves without a check. Their name was removed from the book of life. God withdrew from them, they became an outcast, traitor, captive, God rejected them and they became spiritually dead. Many churches around us are spiritually dead. They base their progress only on their numerical strength and the size of their church building, which is partially right. Unfortunately, God look first at the spiritual life of the ministers and the members, not the size of the congregation only. You can do everything possible to gather cloud but if you cannot feed them spiritually, you are overseeing a dead church and a sinful congregation.

There are pastors who can break any standing law of God, bribe people that matters to pastor big branch in the city. Some general overseers, church founders and leaders enter into cult, witchcraft group and covenant with the devil to get big crowd. But they do not have the grace to preach or teach God's word with power that can produce right result. Such pastors cannot produce mature ministry, good leaders and holy ministers. They have the grammar and can quote many bible passages but they will never produce God-fearing leaders. All the pastors under them will be fake, the children of the devil. Some overseer's mission and purpose of ministry may be just to make name, gather crowd, and compete with other great ministers in the land. Because of this mind, they may make one simple mistake and enter into the pathway of death. Because of that wrong motive, they will not have the patient to wait for God or train ministers. They do not have the fruit of the spirit, though they have the anointing. Anointing without the fruit of the spirit may help you to gather cloud but you will not be patient to train ministers. You will be forced to use any available minister who has no foundation like you.

Others are not called to oversee a church but because of pride, inexperience, anointing and praise of men, they will open up a church.

People like them will gather around them and make them their leader. He will start a church without experience, training and trained ministers. Such minister will manage a dead church, sinful congregation and carnal ministers. If you have a prayer ministry, praise ministry or deliverance ministry without ministers who can preach and teach, you will produce a dead church.

Beating drums, singing, clapping, jumping under fire prayers, shaking and dancing are not a sign of fire in the church. It is only true teaching that new babies can be born into God's family, not prayer or deliverance. After preaching also, those who are born again will grow and mature through the teaching ministry. New people, born again babies can mature from milk to strong meat. The next is disciplining, which is more than teaching. The great strength of any church is its Christian community life, where all learn from one another. The new convert draw strength from the life of the matured ones and grow to maturity, together under ministers who bears the fruit of the Spirit. It is through this growth to maturity that prayer can work and deliverance produced true deliverance. The problem with many ministries who gather cloud today is lack of preaching ministers, teaching ministers and the absence of the fruits of the Holy Spirit.

Jumping into prayer and deliverance without preaching, teaching and discipleship will produce sinning and unrighteous congregation. That was the problem of the church in Sardis.

'And you, being dead in your sins and the uncircumcision of your flesh, hath he quickened together with him, having forgiven you all trespasses' (Colossians 2:13).

'But she that liveth in pleasure is dead while she liveth' (1 Timothy 5:6).

An unbroken minister, uncircumcised in the heart will not help a newborn baby in Christ to mature. He cannot give what he does not have. The ministers in Sardis were uncircumcised, carnal, living unforgiving spirits life. The members copied the same lifestyle and the church became a dead congregation. Their pastors were living in pleasure, so the members copied the same way of life and they became a sinful dead church.

'Wherefore he saith, Awake thou that sleepest, and arise from the dead, and Christ shall give thee light' (Ephesians 5:14).

'It was meet that we should make merry, and be glad: for this thy brother was dead, and is alive again; and was lost, and is found' (Luke 15:32).

They lack preaching ministers, teaching leaders to awake them from sleep in sin or show them light. All the members were at the same level with their pastors. They were in darkness and none have light to lead others out of darkness. They were all dead and lost, so none had the ministry of seeking the lost to found the lost. That is why they were called dead church, they were dead in sin.

'The man that wandereth out of the way of understanding shall remain in the congregation of the dead' (*Proverbs 21:16*).

A church that lack godly preachers, teachers, and discipleship ministers will oppress their members. An oppressing minister will produce members who are wicked, selfish and poor spiritually, though they may be rich physically. And because they were deceived to believe that they were making progress. The average church members in Sardis were very rich financially and materially and as a result, they have self-confidence.

SELF-CONFIDENT CHURCH

Secondly, they were self-confident. The members of the church in Sardis were happy to be called Christians, followers of Christ but they were not aware that Christ does not recognize them. Their work and activities does not please Christ or honor Him. They do not care about their character, what people say about them or even God's word. What they want to see is the material blessings among them. They were so proud and confident that once they belong to the church, they are satisfied. They were happy, testifying of their material blessings without considering the absence of God in their material blessings or the absence of God in their midst (*see* Revelation 3:1).

'Better is the poor that walketh in his uprightness, than he that is perverse in his ways, though he be rich' (*Proverbs 28:6*).

The death in their midst killed good marriage, godly peace, joy, happiness and their spiritual life but they were deceived to believe that once they are blessed materially, there was nothing wrong. They separate, divorce, re-marry and fight over nothing. Their problem, deceit did not start physically but spiritual. They were deceived from the heart and the devil made a fool of them. They needed deliverance but they were not aware because of the material things around them. There are people who think that progress is based only in the acquiring of material things. The members of the church in Sardis had every physical blessing but there was no God in them. Christ was not in their gatherings, prayers, deliverances operations, praises, testimonies and all their activities, yet they were satisfied.

'Ye have plowed wickedness, ye have reaped iniquity; ye have eaten the fruit of lies: because thou didst trust in thy way, in the multitude of thy mighty men' (Hosea 10:13).

They can do any kind of wickedness to prosper, come to church and give testimony. They are very strong hearted in evil acts, witchcraft and iniquity, yet they have confidence. They prosper in business through lies, bribery, murder but they did not see anything wrong in them. Once they need anything, they go after it and they do not mind committing any sin to get their way. Great people in their midst, so to say were great because they could manipulate others, have their way without minding the consequences.

They broke God's word, despise the right way of life and do whatever pleases them without minding God. They roar in the midst of church members, in church service and their speeches promote wickedness. Their testimonies are full of revenge, evil acts and destructions. Their confidence is that whatever they do, once they belong to this powerful church, rich church, popular church, they were favored.

A man therefore can suddenly rise as a leader, pastor or members of the board because he is very rich. Their recognition and position are rated because their tithes, offering, special thanksgiving, personal seed of faith to the pastor over them are greater than others. They were judged and recognized according to how rich they are, not how spiritually. How they made money, get rich does not matter, what matters is how much seed you are able to sow. You receive blessings, prayers from the pastor based on the amount of money you bring to support the church. Some of them engage in wrong business, armed robbery, frauds, drugs and rituals but they are famous in the church. The pastor assures them of God's mercy as long as they bring their tithes every Sunday. They were so confident that no matter what they do, once the pastor prays for them, they are free. So, they break down every rule; despise God's word and waste human life with impunity.

By the way they lived their lives; many strange problems came into the church. Demons attached to their evil acts brought strange fire, problems into the lives of weak members. Many evil spirits defiled the characters of the majority of the church members. The church was brought down by the devil spiritually. They were deceived and removed from God's presence without their knowledge.

'And he spake this parable unto certain, which trusted in themselves that they were righteous, and despised others: Two men went up into the temple to pray; the one a Pharisee, and the other a publican. The Pharisee stood and prayed thus with himself, God, I thank thee, that I am not as other

*men are, extortioners, unjust, adulterers, or even as this
publican. I fast twice in the week, I give tithes of all that I
possess. And the publican, standing afar off, would not lift
up so much as his eyes unto heaven, but smote upon his
breast, saying, God be merciful to me a sinner. I tell you, this
man went down to his house justified rather than the other:
for every one that exalteth himself shall be abased; and he
that humbleth himself shall be exalted' (Luke 18:9-14).*

Their health, business, marriages and job began to have problems. They
ran to the pastor, church and they were deceived repeatedly. Instead of
preaching to them, teaching them the way back to God, they told them
to sow seed. When their problems increased, they told them to sow
more seeds, pray more or go for deliverance upon deliverances. This
continued until some head pastors made their members to lose all their
properties. Others emptied their account and became poor. Some died
in their poverty while few survived as poor members. They were
thought how to live in poverty and make heaven without repentance
and restitutions. Others were taught on how to pray violent prayers, live
by faith without God in their lives. Others were told that why their
business collapsed is because God called them into the ministry of
deliverance.

Today, many of them with demons are delivering others while they are
not delivered. They were taught on the principles of deliverance without
being born again. They attend bible schools, school of deliverance,
school of prayer and many others but they are not born again. Though

they can pray, prophecy and see vision, their source is Satan who has deceived them. They do things in the extreme and practice witchcraft without knowing. Some of them go to the extreme to preach holiness but their holiness is not holy. They are not born again or know the way of Christ. The worst deceit or ignorance is when you are not aware of it. They are so confident in what they are doing without knowing that they were ignorant, wrong and rejected.

'Ye worship ye know not what: we know what we worship: for salvation is of the Jews' (John 4:22).

So many church members in Sardis were happy in their riches, poverty, and deceit and confident without God. Some were without God. Some were happy because that is their father's church. But all their confident in worship and whatever they have were vanity. They think they are better than others because of where they worship. They were deceived by multiple activities and fake assurances from the leaders.

Everyone struggle to obtain certificate to function, belong or recognized from school of prayer, deliverance, prophesy and others. They were ordained by men but rejected by God. They had names everywhere but no life from God. They were confident because they bore the name of Christians, they did not recognize the absence of the life, love and nature of Christ in them. They were self-satisfied church, merrily going along the broad way but they were walking corps before God.

'And unto the angel of the church in Sardis write; These things saith he that hath the seven Spirits of God, and the seven stars; I know thy works, that thou hast a name that thou livest, and art dead... Remember therefore how thou hast received and heard, and hold fast, and repent. If therefore thou shalt not watch, I will come on thee as a thief, and thou shalt not know what hour I will come upon thee' (Revelation 3:1; 3).

Some true believers among them were carried away, mixed up, backslide and joined them. They became formal in singing, praising, in worship and in deliverances without God. They had the written word but not living Lord and they were satisfied. God warned the true believers among them who were being carried away to look back how they started to remember how they started. To remember how they received Christ and His word. How they heard God's word and hold fast and repent.

'For because thou hast trusted in thy works and in thy treasures, thou shalt also be taken: and Chemosh shall go forth into captivity with his priests and his princes together' (Jeremiah 48:7).

He warned them not to be carried away by the polluted riches and anointing of sinners among them. They were deceived to believe that riches, power can be gotten wrongly and enjoyed. They were satisfied without God's presence. Their trust is in the multitude of their treasures without divine presence and approval.

THEY WERE SELF-DELUDED AND INDULGENT

Thirdly, they were self-deluded and self-indulgent. The few contending believers among them were warned to be watchful, and to keep what they have. Christ is sounding the same warning to everyone today. You must be watchful not to be carried away by sinful deceived members in our midst. You must be watchful not to enter into competition with anyone. You must be watchful not to feel inferior or frustrated because of their riches. You must be watchful not to dress like them, talk like them or conduct yourself like them.

'Be watchful, and strengthen the things, which remain, that are ready to die: for I have not found thy works perfect before God. Remember therefore how thou hast received and heard, and hold fast, and repent. If therefore thou shalt not watch, I will come on thee as a thief, and thou shalt not know what hour I will come upon thee. Thou hast a few names even in Sardis, which have not defiled their garments; and they shall walk with me in white: for they are worthy' (<u>Revelation 3:2-4</u>).

You must be watchful not to lose what you have already, your salvation and relationship with Christ. You must not compare yourself or do as they do. You may be in the same group, prayer team, singing group but you must be watchful not to join their evil ways. If you have joined, repent quickly, urgently and come back to God. Christ is telling the few members who were still in faith then and now to keep fighting and to live right. Let your garment, thoughts not be defiled because of the way they live their lives. Do not be carried away because of their big testimonies, houses, cars and boastings. Keep your heart clean so that you will walk with Christ in white.

> 'But be ye doers of the word, and not hearers only, deceiving your own selves. For if any be a hearer of the word, and not a doer, he is like unto a man beholding his natural face in a glass: For he beholdeth himself, and goeth his way, and straightway forgetteth what manner of man he was' (James 1:22-24).

Christ's letter reads, be watchful, keep my word, and obey my commandments. Do not follow them in disobedience, evil plans, and sinful lifestyle. You may keep fellowshipping with them if you must, but keep my word. Do not follow them to hear my word in every gathering without acting on them. Hear and do as I commanded and never follow them in wrong doings. Avoid the way they do business, get rich without obeying my word. Christ is saying, get married, buy cars and build houses but avoid breaking my law because you must do those things. You can look for job, get job, work in an office but avoid the wrong way of sinners. Do not follow them to disobey my words, insist on doing the right thing everywhere. Christ's letter is straight, simple and direct, keeps my words. His letter says, many people, though not all who hears my word, preach my words, sing with my words, conduct deliverances are deceivers.

They hear but they do not obey, they are not doers of my words, they only hear. It is possible to go to bible school, learn how to preach without having the power to do what you tell others to do. In Sardis church, many preach, teach but they lack power to obey. They are trained to preach, teach and pray but they lack the power to put in practice what they teach others. They take ministry as a means of survival, not service to God. They preach holiness but lack the power to live holy. They preach deliverance but they live in sin and lack the ability to deliver self. They preach fasting, give you reasons why you must fast, the results of fasting but they lack the power to fast. They receive tithes, seeds of faith and become rich materially but they are poor spiritually. They live in immorality, adultery, anger, envy, jealous and wickedness, yet they preach deliverance. They look at you and tell you the secrets of your life, everything about your past, present and future but they lack power to stop fornication, lies, anger and all the works of flesh.

'And he spake a parable unto them, saying, The ground of a certain rich man brought forth plentifully: And he thought within himself, saying, What shall I do, because I have no room where to bestow my fruits? And he said, This will I do: I will pull down my barns, and build greater; and there will

I bestow all my fruits and my goods. And I will say to my soul, Soul, thou hast much goods laid up for many years; take thine ease, eat, drink, and be merry. But God said unto him, Thou fool, this night thy soul shall be required of thee: then whose shall those things be, which thou hast provided? So is he that layeth up treasure for himself, and is not rich toward God' (Luke 12:16-21).

They plan how to get money from people in a wrong way. They use prophecy, covetous preaching and witchcraft to achieve their selfishness. They plan how to get what you have, take away your riches without involving God. They use God's Word to make money, enrich themselves, manipulate others but they keep God away from their lives. They have massive wealth through evil means of wealth creations and built greater bans without involving God. They operate fat bank account; home and abroad, build bans here and there without considering God in their actions. They gather wealth through evil means, break God's law and enrich themselves with God's name. They laid down much goods for themselves, children, born and unborn for many generation with the sweats of the poor.

They bewitch members, take their money, their labors, they eat, drink and merry without God. They claim to be gifted in raising fund, not for God's project but for personal use. They think they are wise, rich and smart but they are fools. They feed their body fat, starve their souls and die spiritually. They think they are protected with great wealth, financial power but they are destroyed by self-indulgence. They are dead spiritually because they prefer self-indulgence to self-denial. They lack self-control, practice sin and abandon themselves to their fleshly desires. They do not have any reason to be happy, yet they move about rejoicing because of the physical blessings that have no God in them. They are self-deluded, self-indulgence without self-control.

'We remember the fish, which we did eat in Egypt freely; the cucumbers, and the melons, and the leeks, and the onions, and the garlick' (Numbers 11:5).

'His watchmen are blind: they are all ignorant, they are all dumb dogs, they cannot bark; sleeping, lying down, loving to slumber. Yea, they are greedy dogs, which can never have enough, and they are shepherds that cannot understand: they all look to their own way, every one for his gain, from his quarter. Come ye, say they, I will fetch wine, and we will fill ourselves with strong drink; and tomorrow shall be as this day, and much more abundant' (Isaiah 56:10-12).

They are happy when they remember how rich they are, how powerful they are in witchcraft but they forget that God is far from them. In their store, bans and accounts are with great storage but God's presence was lacking. Their leaders, watchmen were blind, ignorant, dumb dogs, sleeping, lying down and loving slumber. They are filled with greed, always seeking to defraud others with God's Word, in the name of

Christianity. They are shepherds but they lack understanding and go their own way, make gains without God. They are filled with programs that will give them more money, fame and glory. They do not care about the welfare of their poor members, sick members and the less privileged ones. The rich despise the poor; deny them of their rights, benefits and entitlements.

'For many walk, of whom I have told you often, and now tell you even weeping, that they are the enemies of the cross of Christ. Whose end is destruction, whose God is their belly, and whose glory is in their shame, who mind earthly things' (Philippians 3:18-19).

True ministers, those with God's call, who live right and serve God, are being persecuted. They placed them in places of suffering, attack their ministry with witchcraft and starve them of fund. They attack the righteous, their livelihood and destroyed the Christians lives of many. They fight against people with genuine faith, divine call and has forced many to abandon God. Christ wrote to the few contending ministers, members to hold their faith and never look back. The neglected and suffering ones who were born again were asked by Christ through the letter to keep living right, hold fast what they have, trust God, be prayerful and watchful.

'And unto the angel of the church in Sardis write; These things saith he that hath the seven Spirits of God, and the seven stars; I know thy works, that thou hast a name that thou livest, and art dead. Be watchful, and strengthen the things, which remain, that are ready to die: for I have not found thy works perfect before God. Remember therefore how thou hast received and heard, and hold fast, and repent. If therefore thou shalt not watch, I will come on thee as a thief, and thou shalt not know what hour I will come upon thee. Thou hast a few names even in Sardis, which have not defiled their garments; and they shall walk with me in white: for they are worthy' (Revelation 3:1-4).*

'But she that liveth in pleasure is dead while she liveth' (1Timothy 5:6).*

Christ reminded the contending members to fight the good fight and never allow anything, even death to deny them of God's reward. They were encouraged to be stronger and keep what they were dong for Christ in all situation. When you get into any place, office, church in any nation, define your assignment, time and job limits. Work with or without reward, or encouragement knowing that if you play your part, God will reward you in due time. Pray that you will not under stay because of attacks, discouragement and the activities of the agent of the devil.

Pray that you will not overstay because of fear of attacks or the promotion from the devil or his agents. Many people were in Sardis but their times have expired. They were afraid that if they leave, they would be attacked or lose what they already have. Others are there because they got promotion outside God's will. Christ told the few believers, whose names were in the book of life not to join the multitudes to do evil, pursue wealth and die spiritually. They must not be defiled or pollute themselves with pleasures. They must not love the world, the things of this world. They must avoid the things of this world that will take them away from divine focus.

They must not allow anything, any person in this world to shift them from focusing into heaven, eternity and heavenly reward. They must not allow their flesh, the vainglory of this world, the lusts of the things of this world to take away God's spirit from them. They must live holy, avoid pride, carnality and things they see, hear, feel or think to shift their faith in God and from God. They must agree with God's word, disagree with anything that disagree with God's word and contend to the end.

'And Jesus answering said unto them, Suppose ye that these Galilaeans were sinners above all the Galilaeans, because they suffered such things? I tell you, Nay: but, except ye repent, ye shall all likewise perish' (Luke 13:2-3).

'And saying, The time is fulfilled, and the kingdom of God is at hand: repent ye, and believe the gospel' (Mark 1:15).

It is better to suffer worse things, go through worse pains and die contending for the faith than to die in sin. It is better to remain with Christ, keep relationship with Him than to compromise. The church in Sardis became sensual, social gathering where people came to show their best designed clothes. Offering time was a time to show new dresses, shoes and golden wristwatches. People's mind was perverted, diverted from the reality.

Times of testimonies, appreciating God were an opportunity to tell lies, pretend and show off. The car park was filled with pride because people just go there to show whose car is the latest, the best. Those who drive small cars were tempted to do anything possible, good or bad to change their cars to belong. The poor ones, the less privileged were nobody and had no place in the church at Sardis. It was worse than worldly normal social club was.

Believers, poor people were nothing because they have no place. Their purpose of going to church, fellowship is to socialize and boast of new things, the latest in the city. They drove God away, despise His servants and destroyed the ministries of greatly destined ministers. The church was dead spiritually and there was no divine presence.

CHRIST'S SOLEMN COMMAND

Children of God are known for their obedient and they obey every command.

> 'Be watchful, and strengthen the things, which remain, that are ready to die: for I have not found thy works perfect before God. Remember therefore how thou hast received and heard, and hold fast, and repent. If therefore thou shalt not watch, I will come on thee as a thief, and thou shalt not know what hour I will come upon thee' (Revelation 3:2-3).

> 'Therefore watch, and remember, that by the space of three years I ceased not to warn every one night and day with tears' (Acts 20:31).

Christ in His letter did not ask them to be watchful; He commanded them to be watchful. Watching over our soul is a commandment. He who watch over his soul, God will watch over other things he has. When danger is coming and before any destruction take place, Christ normally warns His followers, give them command to escape destruction. The letter to the church in Sardis was a sound of alarm to alert believers to avoid the impending danger. It is a deliverance letter to all believers in Sardis at that time and to all believers of all ages, everywhere today, tomorrow and forever. In time of flood, when most houses have been flooded and ours still stand in danger of being flooded, we must be alerted. At the time of this letter, many churches worldwide have been taken away by the flood of worldliness, pursuit of riches and pleasures without God. The letters to the seven churches in Asia at that time was letters of deliverance for the remnants. The command to be watchful is not optional but for all of us who are alive today. You have to be watchful, be prayerful and determined to follow through to the end. You must be strong, no matter the pleasures before you.

'Watch ye, stand fast in the faith, quit you like men, be strong' (1Corinthians 16:13).

'Wherefore lift up the hands which hang down, and the feeble knees; And make straight paths for your feet, lest that which is lame be turned out of the way; but let it rather be healed. Follow peace with all men, and holiness, without which no man shall see the Lord: Looking diligently lest any man fail of the grace of God; lest any root of bitterness springing up trouble you, and thereby many be defiled; Lest there be any fornicator, or profane person, as Esau, who for one morsel of meat sold his birthright. For ye know how that afterward, when he would have inherited the blessing, he was rejected: for he found no place of repentance, though he sought it carefully with tears' (Hebrews 12:12-17).

As we watch, we must remember the people who have passed through this way before us. We must remember that this is the last days and the danger of compromise is greatly increasing. We must observe the signs, the warning and dangers of compromise. We must remember that Aaron was called by God and he answered. He valiantly stood with Moses in the ministry before Pharaoh of Egypt in Egypt. He later under great pressures, compromised, built idol and worshipped it.

Many pastors, their members who once stood with God are compromising. Some have compromised in moral standard to get material prosperity and solve immediate pressing needs. Others because of the problems and enemies before them and their determination to win at all cost has compromised. They backslide, won their competitors and died without repentance. Others want to draw cloud, get more members, helpers, to attain certain achievements. They compromised, went into the battlefield and died without God. Others because of tender appeal, made to their needs and because they must meet those needs, they compromised. You remember Solomon, the chosen king, the wisest king and a true worshipper of God. Latter in his life, because he did not take God's warning and command serious, he compromised. He listened to outlandish women and they caused him to compromise and backslide. In many churches today, some pastors are surrounded by influential women they cannot say no to. They bow to women's requests for ceremonies and ungodly request that demanded for the heads of God's ministers. They wrongly transfer ministers, kill their anointing and destroy God's call because of the requests from outlandish women

'But king Solomon loved many strange women, together with the daughter of Pharaoh, women of the Moabites,

Ammonites, Edomites, Zidonians, and Hittites; Of the nations concerning which the LORD said unto the children of Israel, Ye shall not go in to them, neither shall they come in unto you: for surely they will turn away your heart after their gods: Solomon clave unto these in love. And he had seven hundred wives, princesses, and three hundred concubines: and his wives turned away his heart. For it came to pass, when Solomon was old, that his wives turned away his heart after other gods: and his heart was not perfect with the LORD his God, as was the heart of David his father. For Solomon went after Ashtoreth the goddess of the Zidonians, and after Milcom the abomination of the Ammonites. And Solomon did evil in the sight of the LORD, and went not fully after the LORD, as did David his father. Then did Solomon build an high place for Chemosh, the abomination of Moab, in the hill that is before Jerusalem, and for Molech, the abomination of the children of Ammon. And likewise did he for all his strange wives, which burnt incense and sacrificed unto their gods' (1Kings 11:1-8).

'Did not Solomon king of Israel sin by these things? Yet among many nations was there no king like him, who was beloved of his God, and God made him king over all Israel: nevertheless even him did outlandish women cause to sin' (Nehemiah 13:26).

Others compromised in unhealthy friendships and unscriptural co-operation with ministers who are in cults. They begin to invite backsliding ministers, enemies of God who prophesy to make money from the members. They preferred ministers with big names and in covenant with demons. They chose to associate, invite and organize programs with people of different conviction; lower moral standard and people begin to doubt their call. Because of money or ignorance, many have compromised by relating with ministers with unsteady principles, unstable doctrines to defile their pulpits.

Others compromised in modification of their original doctrinal stand on marriage, modesty and things that does not conform to the word. Today in many churches, people because of the fear of leadership, persecution and what people will say, have compromised.

In Sardis church, many backslide and compromised because they want to belong. They prefer to ordain men of wealth than to ordain confirmed God's ministers. Others because they want to make it quick, get large congregation, pastor the biggest church in the city has compromised and joined cults. They want power to perform miracles, heal the sick but do not have the fruit of the spirit to wait for true anointing.

They rushed out, went into the dark and were empowered by evil spirits. They want quick success and achievement and they compromised. Today, they have achieved what they call success, reached man made goal but they are demonized by destructive demons inside them, they try to deliver others even with demons inside them. They are deceived and are being used to deceive others. The warning and command from Christ to you is watch and remember.

Remember that many are already in bondage because of entering cult, idolatry, evil influence, compromise on moral standard. Remember that they are in troubles today because they compromised on moral standard to gain material things, win over a competitor, reach goals for achievement and become great in life. Remember that keeping evil wealthy relationship has caused many to compromise.

Remember that pride, the inability for some great ministers to accept their faults, apologize and restitute has killed them and took them to hell fire. Christ gave us this letter to deliver us from being afraid of the persecution we must go through, suffering we must go through and trials we must go through. This warning and commands is coming to us as a letter of deliverance.

We must not do anything, permit anyone to deliver us from what we must pass through to get the right blessings, right anointing, and direct empowerment from above. This letter of deliverance is coming to you now to warn you not to lose your original true perspective, which is to please God alone, serve Him alone and live for His glory alone. This command is coming to us at this time to help us to prefer godly men to ungodly men or people of wealth without character. We must remember to live right in the midst of multiple evil influences, pressure groups in the church, place of work, school and in the market places.

We must learn how to say no to opposite sex brought into our lives by the devil to overthrow our faith in Christ. We must be warned and take

262 • Prayer M. Madueke

this letter very serious to overcome the pressure groups under the influence of the devil. Pressure groups, energized by the devil and self, who judge things carnally by outward appearance. This is what killed the church in Sardis and God is warning us to desist from it.

You must watch, stand fast in the faith, quit like men and be strong. The time we are in is not the time to pity our body or satisfy the demand within us at all cost. It is a time to say no and refuse to crave for position at all cost, popularity and praise of men. It is a time to say no to any demand in us to abandon the praise of God to men. It is a time to say no to any contract, wealth and achievement without God's approval.

It is a time to watch every offer, stand fast in faith, quit like men and be strong for God and not in wrong things. This is time to move forward and worship only God without any condition. It is a time to take stand for God and make our paths straight. It is a time to humble ourselves, make peace with all men, including our worse enemies. It is a time to live holy, imitate Christ and pray for victory over every trouble.

It is a time to rise, say no to fornication, ungodly lifestyles, and stand for God everywhere. It is a time to control our appetite, live a sacrificial life and self-denial. It is also a time to be watchful, strengthen the weak, the fainting members and encourage sinners to repent. It is a time to remember how we started this journey, how we received Christ and held fast our faith. This command is from Christ who died for the church and must not be neglected but to be held seriously. To neglect such command is to forsake life and chose death and chose to spend eternity in hell fire.

THE SECOND COMING OF CHRIST

The rapture, the time when Christ comes for the saints, can take place any moment from now, for the saints and can take place right away-now. But Christ needed to tell the church in Sardis that after the rapture, there is a second coming. The second coming of Christ or the Second Advent is the time Christ comes with the saints to the earth. The Second Advent will take place immediately after the great tribulation.

'Now we beseech you, brethren, by the coming of our Lord Jesus Christ, and by our gathering together unto him... For the mystery of iniquity doth already work: only he who now letteth will let, until he be taken out of the way. And then shall that wicked be revealed, whom the Lord shall consume with the spirit of his mouth, and shall destroy with the brightness of his coming' (2 Thessalonians 2:1; 7-8).

It is a time all saints will gather together with Christ after great tribulation. By that time, Christ will come to the earth with His saints that were raptured. Once the rapture takes place, the great tribulation will start and last for seven years. That is what Paul spoke of as revealing the wicked and consuming him with the spirit of his mouth. It is the judgment of the wicked to give way for the second coming of the Lord with His saints. Christ needed to tell the suffering saints in Sardis His program for them to encourage them to be steadfast.

'Remember therefore how thou hast received and heard, and hold fast, and repent. If therefore thou shalt not watch, I will come on thee as a thief, and thou shalt not know what hour I will come upon thee' (Revelation 3:3).

They needed to know that their suffering and holding unto the end is not in vain. He told them to watch over their soul and to contend for their faith to the end. Christians must not give the devil any moment of their lives with unrighteousness. The reason given by Christ is that His coming will be like that of a thief at night. It is going to be imminent, unannounced and sudden.

'But of that day and hour knoweth no man, no, not the angels of heaven, but my Father only. But as the days of Noe were, so shall also the coming of the Son of man be. For as in the days that were before the flood they were eating and drinking, marrying and giving in marriage, until the day that Noe entered into the ark, And knew not until the flood came, and took them all away; so shall also the coming of the Son of man be' (Matthew 24:36-39).

The day, the hour of His second coming and the rapture is not known and no man, not even angel knows the time, day and hour. This calls for serious watch every moment without compromise or lose life. God is warning us through this letter to avoid what happened to the people in the days of Noah from being repeated. This letter is filled with love from Christ to every one of us. God used Noah to preach in his days to warn sinners but they rejected his preaching and despised his words.

Today, God is speaking not through Noah or prophets but through his only son. It will be more destructive and woeful to joke with this letter of deliverance. Few days before the flood of Noah's days, the devil released great wealth on earth. Testimonies of unbelievers increased and every need was released. There was abundant provision of good things of every need. They were mocking Noah when all his life's savings was invested for the building of the ark of salvation. The devil released money into the ministry of unbelievers and there was prosperity like never before in the land.

The unbelievers prospered left and right without restriction. Business opportunities increased and the focus was on the evil activities. Things that will distract people from listening to the message of Noah increased. The devil released marriages he was sitting upon. They despised Noah, his ministry and the preaching of righteousness. Everyone was engaged, too busy for God and Noah was alone in his ministry of righteous living.

Maybe that is your picture in the ministry, the village or city where you live. The message of salvation, sanctification and pursuit for godliness, true power has been abandoned. People are running after prophets and ministers with healing power. They despise righteousness, righteous preaching and run after ministers with fake anointing. That was the condition of the church in Sardis, and that is the condition in our churches today.

> 'Thine enemies roar in the midst of thy congregations; they set up their ensigns for signs.... They said in their hearts, Let us destroy them together: they have burned up all the synagogues of God in the land. We see not our signs: there is no more any prophet: neither is there among us any that knoweth how long' (Psalm 74:4; 8-9).

God's enemies in the name of ministry have taken over the pulpits in our generation. They received fake prophetic power, defiled healings and polluted miracles. Power and prosperity to divert members from hearing and doing God's will. They changed God's true miracles, signs and wonders with demonic transfers to deceive the mind of the simple. They burned up the churches in the land with fake fire. They bewitched people to follow them as they distributed defiled blessings to distract people from God.

Marriage is good, eating and drinking is good but any condition attached to it against God's word is not acceptable. Christ's letter to the few remaining contending believers in Sardis is to remind them of what happened in the days of Noah. The fake prosperity, defiled blessings, contaminated marriage breakthrough they got took them away from the true gospel. Deliverance focus for healing, prosperity and many blessing that will not touch souls is fake and unprofitable.

Fake preaching, prophecies, prosperity without righteousness and incomplete deliverance has taken away many people from God. Christ's letter of deliverance to the church in Sardis for the few contending believers is to ignore every fake and focus on the good relationship with God. They are to join the preachers of righteousness and build the ark of salvation.

> 'And the LORD said unto Noah, Come thou and all thy house into the ark; for thee have I seen righteous before me in this generation... And Noah went in, and his sons, and his wife, and his sons' wives with him, into the ark, because of the waters of the flood' (Genesis 7:1; 7).

The letter that God wrote to Noah was read to all but few heard it and acted upon it. God does not work with crowd. He works with few that hear His words and acts on them. Don't be deceived because of the ministers that multiply programs to deceive people with demonic deliverances and prosperity without God. The letter of deliverance from Christ to the church in Sardis is for all but only the few that act on it will be delivered. You may not be alive in the second coming but death can come anytime. Are you ready to meet God if you die now?

The day Noah went into the ark with his family, the water of judgment was released. Every human investment was affected and no human being of every class was spared. The people that died every day in the plane crash, road accidents and deaths in the hospitals were not told of their day of death. When God released judgment in the days of Noah, the only people that survived were righteous people inside the Ark. Marriage is good, prosperity is good, deliverance is good but they must come from God if we must partake in the second coming.

'But covet earnestly the best gifts: and yet shew I unto you a more excellent way' (1Corinthians 12:31).

'And now abideth faith, hope, charity, these three; but the greatest of these is charity' (1Corinthians 12:31).

I said it before but let me repeat myself. Any gift, be it healing, prophecy, etc., that has any trace of anger, greed, pride, immorality, jealousy, covetousness, love of money or any work of the flesh in the life of the owner is lighter than nothing, unprofitable and worse than the worse. The world is filled with counterfeit and the only way to discern counterfeit is to check the character of the container.

'Be ye therefore ready also: for the Son of man cometh at an hour when ye think not' (Luke 12:40).

'For yourselves know perfectly that the day of the Lord so cometh as a thief in the night' (1Thessalonians 5:2).

'Behold, I come as a thief. Blessed is he that watcheth, and keepeth his garments, lest he walk naked, and they see his shame' (Revelation 16:15).

Christ's letter to you and me for our deliverance is that our thinking may fail us but He will not fail us. If you ignore your thinking and believe Christ, live right, no matter the hour, you will not miss it. If you remain righteous every hour, no matter your problem now, true deliverance will come at the hour you think not. Deliverance that comes through righteousness cannot expire, it is everlasting.

You do not need to bother yourself for anything. If you meet up with God's requirement, your deliverance will come; no power can postpone your deliverance in the midst of righteousness and deliverance prayer. But the problem with many deliverance ministers and ministry is too much prayer in the absence of righteous living. To watch is to examine yourself every day to check if you still keep relationship with Christ. It means to live above sin, to live in the will of God. It helps to keep our garment clean and make us not to walk naked or to be put to shame.

'Let your moderation be known unto all men. The Lord is at hand' (Philippians 4:5).

'For yet a little while, and he that shall come will come, and will not tarry' (<u>Hebrews 10:37</u>).

'Behold, I come quickly: hold that fast which thou hast, that no man take thy crown' (<u>Revelation 3:11</u>).

To watch means to do things to the glory of God, in moderation in the sight of God and men. You may be the richest person in your church, do things in moderation. Do not over step, do everything to the glory of God. Christ can come as you are about to give bribe, commit immorality or sin. You can die in the very act of lies, cheat or at the point of evil negotiation. You can drop dead as you are about to leave the scene of sin, the hotel room.

Anything can happen when you never or least expect them to take place. Christ's letter is watch, remain righteous, steadfast and contend to the end. Do not compromise your faith for anything on earth. For sinners and backsliders who linger in sin and negligent in watching, He will come on them as a thief. Great shall be their loss and sorrows.

COUNSEL FOR SPOTLESS CHRISTIANS

The details activities of everyone in the church, everywhere on earth are exposed before God. He looked into the lives of the multitude members of the people in church at Sardis and discovered that many were no longer in faith. Few names among them have not defiled their garments. To such people, He assured them that if they continue, they would not regret their decision.

> 'Thou hast a few names even in Sardis, which have not defiled their garments; and they shall walk with me in white: for they are worthy' (_Revelation 3:4_).
>
> 'The LORD is good, a strong hold in the day of trouble; and he knoweth them that trust in him' (Nahum 1:7).
>
> 'I am the good shepherd, and know my sheep, and am known of mine' (_John 10:14_).

God is so good that He will not allow any troubled Christian who trusts in Him to perish in his trouble. If your decision for Christ reached your heart unto death at all cost, you will not regret it. If the devil knows that you trust God beyond your flesh, he will not trouble you to an extent. Christ's letter to the church in Sardis was to encourage them to remain faithful, obedient to God's word unto the end. Any believer who wishes to get true deliverance from Christ must submit totally to Him in everything. You must be spotless and maintain relationship with Him in everything.

> 'Nevertheless the foundation of God standeth sure, having this seal, The Lord knoweth them that are his. And, Let everyone that nameth the name of Christ depart from iniquity' (2 Timothy 2:19).

> 'Pure religion and undefiled before God and the Father is this, To visit the fatherless and widows in their affliction, and to keep himself unspotted from the world' (James 1:27).

> 'But and if ye suffer for righteousness' sake, happy are ye: and be not afraid of their terror, neither be troubled' (1Peter 3:14).

To please Christ, you must submit to His standard by departing from every form of iniquity with a single mind to please Him. Suffering for the sake of Christ is a thing of joy and no believer must deny Christ when he is suffering for being obedient. No Christian has any excuse to defile his robe of righteousness for any reason. In the worst situation, believers must remain clean, righteous and worthy to the end.

> 'He that overcometh, the same shall be clothed in white raiment; and I will not blot out his name out of the book of life, but I will confess his name before my Father, and before

his angels. He that hath an ear, let him hear what the Spirit saith unto the churches' (Revelation 3:5-6).

The backslidden believers in Sardis think that to be an overcomer, you must get rich at all cost, even if it means breaking God's law. In Sardis church, many were deceived to believe that making money by breaking God's word is being on overcomer. There are pastors who think that if they know the big names in the city, invite the most powerful ministers to minister in their church, they are overcomers.

Others think that once they build house, big cathedral and drive the best car, they are overcomers. They do every bad thing, horrible things to achieve the above. Others think that if they have power to heal the sick, conduct deliverance and cast out demons, they are overcomers. Others think that getting married, obtaining a certificate and working in a particular office makes them overcomers.

Others enter into cult, witchcraft group and evil organization to be powerful and as a result, they think, they are overcomers. Others think that seeing, hearing voices and prophesying accurately make them overcomers. They do everything possible to get the above without considering God's word and they come out and believe that they are overcomers. Whatever you have now, you are pursuing but you are not born again, you may get it but your soul will suffer eternally in hell fire.

Anything you have gotten but you still live in sin, you are in no way close to being an overcomer. True overcomers overcome sin, live above sin, and other things bows on their own. The greatest achievement of overcomers is victory over sin and that will write your name in the book of life. Once your name gets into God's book, every problems will rise against you but that will make Christ to confess you, bring your case file before God and His angels.

> 'And whosoever was not found written in the book of life was cast into the lake of fire' (_Revelation 20:15_).

> 'And there shall in no wise enter into it anything that defileth, neither whatsoever worketh abomination, nor maketh a lie: but they which are written in the Lamb's book of life' (_Revelation 21:27_).

Therefore, all overcomers name are written down in God's book of life. That is the start of your overcomer ship. Between the time your name is written in the book of life and the time Christ will confess you before God, you need to fight some battles. Christ's letter is saying to every overcomer, be patient, I am introducing you, confessing you before God and His angels. As God receives your case file, and there is no defilement or anything that is abominable on your life, you will be rewarded. That is why every believer needs to bear God's fruits.

> 'Envyings, murders, drunkenness, revellings, and such like: of the which I tell you before, as I have also told you in time

past, that they which do such things shall not inherit the kingdom of God. But the fruit of the Spirit is love, joy, peace, longsuffering, gentleness, goodness, faith' (<u>Galatians 5:21-22</u>).

As a believer, Christ's letter of deliverance to you is to wait. You need to bear God's Spirit under any situation and be steadfast. No matter what you are going through, when you remember that your case file is before God and His angel, joy and peace comes up into your mind. The knowledge that your case file is with the Almighty God will help you manifest long-suffering, gentleness, goodness, faith, meekness, temperance and all the life of Christ. It will give you hope and calmness. The knowledge that very soon, no matter the pains, attacks, once God minutes into your file, everything will be over. The information that God is handling your case will move you to ignore every evil presence. It will move you into prayer and gives you the power to believe that very soon, your deliverance will come.

'And at that time shall Michael stand up, the great prince which standeth for the children of thy people: and there shall be a time of trouble, such as never was since there was a nation even to that same time: and at that time thy people shall be delivered, every one that shall be found written in the book' (<u>Daniel 12:1</u>).

'Notwithstanding in this rejoice not, that the spirits are subject unto you; but rather rejoice, because your names are written in heaven' (Luke 10:20).

When you have a part in the book of life, you will not be afraid of even death. If you are aware that your case file is before God and that Michael, the great Prince is standing for you, no deliverance will be impossible for you. You may have a time of trouble, you may enter into great problem but once your name is in God's book, you will be delivered. As long as your name is remaining in the book of life, no trouble, problem will consume you. You will be delivered. That was what Christ told the church in Sardis and that is what He is telling us today.

The greatest enemy in life is not your enemy, it's not your problem, but anything that will take your name out from the book of life. The worse problem in life is not to conquer death, Ebola or the entire incurable problem put together. The greatest problem of anyone, all believers is anything, or power that can take your name out of the book of life. Whatever is happening to you now, sickness, poverty, hardship or the worst problem on earth, if you allow your name to remain in the book of life, you will be delivered.

'And the LORD said unto Moses, Whosoever hath sinned against me, him will I blot out of my book' (Exodus 32:33).

'And I intreat thee also, true yokefellow, help those women which labored with me in the gospel, with Clement also, and with other my fellow laborers, whose names are in the book of life' (Philippians 4:3).

'To the general assembly and church of the firstborn, which are written in heaven, and to God the Judge of all, and to the spirits of just men made perfect' (Hebrews 12:23).

You may be under terrible suffering, the worse persecution and under the oppression of Pharaoh, if they cannot take your name out of the book of life, they cannot stop your deliverance. Any enemy, forces of darkness that cannot take your name from the book of life cannot stop your deliverance.

The weapon that the devil uses to take away peoples name out of God's book of life is sin. In the Sardis church, the devil used spiritual death to remove their names from the book of life.

In Thyatira, he used filthy prophetess, her false teaching and seduction to remove their names from the book of life. Whoever, whatever cannot remove your name from the book of life cannot stop your deliverance. If your name is in the book of life, you will receive help, deliverance and freedom from every trouble. Is your name in the book of life or just in a church book? If your answer is no, you need to repent, confess your sins, forsake them and dedicate your life to Christ. Ask Him to write your name in the book of life. If your name is in the book of life, then know that you are qualified for deliverance.

SELECTED DECREES

DECREE TO PREPARE FOR YOUR END

Almighty God, fill me with your righteousness and empower me to contend to the end, in the name of Jesus. Every organized darkness threatening my faith in Christ, be frustrated. Any root of sin in my life, be uprooted by the blood of Jesus, in the name of Jesus. Every enemy of my relationship with Christ, be frustrated, in the name of Jesus. Blood of Jesus, flow into my foundation and destroy the root of sin. Almighty God, give me enough grace to stand with Christ to the end, in the name of Jesus.

I receive power never to run away from identifying with Christ forever, in the name of Jesus. Anything in my past, present and future, militating against my relationship with Christ, perish. I refuse to run away from the persecution I must pass through for Christ's sake, in the name of Jesus. Almighty God, empower me to be an encouragement to the body of Christ. Power to end my life in Christ and make heaven, possess me. Any evil character assigned to separate me from Christ, die, in the name of Jesus. Father Lord, help me never to deny Christ. Power to contend for my faith in Christ till I die, possess me, in the name of Jesus. Anything from the devil and his agent, designed to separate me from Christ, I reject you, in the name of Jesus.

DECREE AGAINST LACK OF KNOWLEDGE

Father Lord, release Your divine wisdom and knowledge into my life, in Jesus' name. O Lord, fill my brain with Your knowledge and power. Blood of Jesus, speak me out of every knowledge that is unprofitable to my life, in the name of Jesus. Every enemy of God's knowledge inside me, I cast you out. Lord Jesus, help me to acquire enough knowledge from above. Father Lord, paralyze every evil imagination working against me, in the name of Jesus.

Every evil mouth opened against God's Word, close by force, in the name of Jesus. I command every knowledge against God's knowledge to die. Any agent of Satan delaying God's program for my life, be frustrated, in the name of Jesus. Fire of God, burn all evil information in my brain to ashes. O Lord, upgrade my brain to accommodate more of Your knowledge, in the name of Jesus.

Every arrow of confusion fired into my brain, I fire you back, in the name of Jesus. Any area of my life that is lacking divine knowledge, receive deliverance. Blood of Jesus, flow into my brain and increase my knowledge, in the name of Jesus. I cast out of my life every enemy of divine knowledge. Any evil spirit that is stealing God's knowledge from my life, I cast your out. O Lord, fill me with Your knowledge, wisdom and power, in the name of Jesus. Every weapon of lack of knowledge in my life, be roasted by fire, in the name of Jesus.

DECREE AGAINST TROUBLES WITHIN

Any agent of Satan assigned to pull down God's children, be frustrated, in the name of Jesus. Almighty God, expose and disgrace every enemy of God's children. Blood of Jesus, energize me to overcome every trouble, in the name of Jesus. Any evil force that is living inside of me, I cast you out, in the name of Jesus. Lord Jesus, deliver me from unfriendly friends. I break every yoke of sin in my life. Any problem in the body of Christ designed to destroy me, die, in the name of Jesus. Father Lord, deliver me from every internal enemy, in the name of Jesus.

Any witch or wizard in our midst, be exposed and disgraced, in the name of Jesus. Any evil counselor that is working against me, be disgraced. Blood of Jesus, speak me out from every trouble, in the name of Jesus. Any strange fire burning inside me, be quenched by force. Every yoke of sin in my life, break to pieces, in the name of Jesus. I walk out from the captivity of internal enemies, in the name of Jesus. You, the enemies in our midst, be frustrated. O Lord, arise and deliver me from the enemies within, in the name of Jesus.

282 • Prayer M. Madueke

DECREE AGAINST EXTERNAL TROUBLES

O Lord, arise and deliver me from the troubles that are bigger than me, in the name of Jesus. Power to confront and conquer every external enemy, possess me. Any evil arrow that is coming from unknown enemy, I fire you back, in the name of Jesus. Any evil force assigned against me from far places, scatter, in the name of Jesus. I command the anointing of external enemies to be terminated. O Lord, give me power to overcome all external enemies, in the name of Jesus. Father Lord, deliver me from evil forces coming against me from all sides. Every enemy that is standing in front of me, behind or back, be wasted, in the name of Jesus.

I destroy every enemy that is spoiling my relationship with God, in the name of Jesus. Blood of Jesus, help me to overcome all external enemies. Every arrow of death that is fired at me, backfire, in the name of Jesus. Any evil spirit that is knocking at my door, be roasted by fire. O Lord, arise and deliver me from external enemies, in the name of Jesus. Let every enemy troubling my life be troubled unto death. Every messenger of disappointment to my life, I reject your message, in the name of Jesus. Father Lord, deliver me from all troubles. Any evil utterance that is assigned to waste my life, expire, in the name of Jesus. O Lord, arise and deliver me from all kinds of trouble, in the name of Jesus.

DECREE AGAINST ALTARS OF SIN

Almighty God, thank You for Your power, in the name of Jesus. Any evil altar that is holding me down, release me by force. Every yoke of sin from any evil altar in my life, break, in the name of Jesus. Any sin that has refused to let me go, release me by force. Every messenger of sin in my life, I reject you and your message, in the name of Jesus. I break and lose myself from altars of sin. Power to say no to all manner of sin, possess me now, in the name of Jesus. Blood of Jesus, speak me out from the power of sin. Any evil altar that is promoting sin in my life, be destroyed, in the name of Jesus.

Every property of sin in my life from evil altars, catch fire, in the name of Jesus.

O Lord, arise and deliver me from the altars of sin, in the name of Jesus. Every dream of sin in my life, die by force. Any judgment against me from altars of sin, I reverse you, in the name of Jesus. I walk out forever from the altar of sin. I break and lose myself from the captivity of sin, in the name of Jesus. Heavenly Father, empower me to say no to sin, in the name of Jesus. You, my body, soul and spirit, I command you to reject sinful lifestyles, in the name of Jesus.

DECREE AGAINST MYSTERIOUS ATTACKS

Heavenly Father, appear and deliver me from every satanic attack, in the name of Jesus. Every unknown problem in my life, be exposed and disgraced. Any strange movement in my life, die by Holy Ghost fire, in the name of Jesus. Any violent demon oppressing my destiny, I cast you out. O God, arise and deliver me from mysterious attacks, in the name of Jesus. Any evil power that is feeding me in my dreams, be destroyed. Let the spirit of darkness assigned to waste my life be disorganized, in the name of Jesus.

Blood of Jesus, flow into my life and capture my destiny, in the name of Jesus. Any satanic department assigned to kill me mysteriously, fail woefully. Father Lord, command Your angels to deliver me from troubles, in the name of Jesus. You, my hidden problems, be exposed and disgraced. Any agent of devil working against my destiny, be frustrated, in the name of Jesus. O Lord, arise and take me away from satanic altars. Fire of God, burn to ashes every enemy that is targeting my sound health, in the name of Jesus. I waste any mysterious attack that is ongoing in my life. Almighty God, take over every area of my life forever, in the name of Jesus. Every yoke of mysterious problems in my life, break by force. Every enemy of my deliverance, you are finished, fail woefully, in the name of Jesus.

DECREE AGAINST POVERTY AND SUFFERING

Every demonic information in my life, be exposed and disgraced, in the name of Jesus. Father Lord, deliver me from every manner of poverty. Lord Jesus, deliver me from every trap I have entered into because of poverty, in the name of Jesus. Any power that is holding me down in poverty, release me by force. You, my mind, walk out from the captivity of poverty, in the name of Jesus. Any suffering I am going through because of the poverty of the mind, stop. Heavenly Father, terminate every suffering in my life by force, in the name of Jesus. Any demon in charge of ignorance in my life, I cast you out. O Lord, deliver any department of my life that is under the captivity of poverty, in the name of Jesus.

Any failure that poverty is keeping in my life, perish. I break satanic bondage I have entered because of poverty, in the name of Jesus. Every good thing that poverty has destroyed in my life, receive life, in the name of Jesus. O Lord, deliver me from rejection poverty has brought into my life. Every anointing of poverty and suffering in my life, break, in the name of Jesus. I break and lose my life from every problem that poverty has brought. Every enemy of prosperity and abundance in my life, die, in the name of Jesus.

I challenge and disgrace poverty and suffering in my life, in the name of Jesus. I dismantle the root of poverty and suffering in my life. Any evil authority that poverty is exercising over my life, die, in the name of Jesus. Heavenly Father, remove the foothold of poverty and suffering in my life. Holy Ghost fire, burn to ashes the seed of poverty in my life, in the name of Jesus. I terminate forever the voice of poverty and suffering in my life, in the name of Jesus. Any messenger of devil attacking me with poverty and suffering, fail woefully Any spirit in my life that is shutting out prosperity, I cast you out, in the name of Jesus. Every agent of poverty and suffering in my life, be exposed and disgraced. Any oppression I am going through because of poverty, be terminated, in the name of Jesus. I withdraw my life from the captivity of poverty and suffering. Every ground I have lost to poverty in my life, I recover you double. Poverty and suffering in any area of my life, abandon me now, in the name of Jesus. Holy Ghost fire, burn to ashes every trace of poverty in my life. I break and lose myself from inherited poverty and lack, in the name of Jesus.

DECREE AGAINST ETERNAL JUDGMENT

Great God, deliver me from the spirit of compromise, in the name of Jesus. Every enemy of truth in my life, I cast you out. I break and loose myself from any evil covenant, in the name of Jesus. Any evil force from my occult background attacking my life, scatter, in the name of Jesus. Almighty God, deliver me from any curse place upon my life, in the name of Jesus.

Every bondage I brought upon my life, break, in the name of Jesus.

Power to say no to sin and evil doctrines, possess me now, in the name of Jesus. Every enemy of my full deliverance, your time is up, perish, in the name of Jesus. Fire of God, burn between me and every enemy of my faith in Christ.

Father Lord, deliver me from every evil soul-tie, in the name of Jesus. Every problem in my life, receive destruction, in the name of Jesus. I command every evil altar in the city to release my destiny, in the name of Jesus.

288 • Prayer M. Madueke

TRUE DELIVERANCE DECREE

Lord Jesus, deliver me from every falsehood, in the name of Jesus. Every arrow of confusion fired against me, back fire, in the name of Jesus. Any false prophet/prophetess attached to my life, be frustrated, in the name of Jesus. Any evil personality controlling my life, be exposed and disgraced, in the name of Jesus. Almighty God, deliver me from every problem in life, in the name of Jesus. Any demonic fear in my life from false prophesies, be destroyed, in the name of Jesus. Everlasting God, control me and bless me with your everlasting word, in the name of Jesus.

THANK YOU!

I wanted to take this opportunity to appreciate you for supporting my ministry and writing career by purchasing my book. I'm a full-time author and every copy of my book bought helps tremendously in supporting my family and that I continue to have the energy and motivation to write. My family and I are very grateful and we don't take your support lightly.

Thank you so much as you spare this precious moment of your time and may God bless you and meet you at every point of your need.

Send me an email on prayermadu@yahoo.com if you need prayers or counsel or you have questions. Better still if you want to be friends with me.

Other Books by Prayer Madueke

1. 100 Days Prayers to Wake Up Your Lazarus
2. 15 Deliverance Steps to Everlasting Life
3. 21/40 Nights of Decrees and Your Enemies Will Surrender
4. 35 Deliverance Steps to Everlasting Rest
5. 35 Special Dangerous Decrees
6. 40 Prayer Giants
7. Alone with God
8. Americans, May I Have Your Attention Please
9. Avoid Academic Defeats
10. Because You Are Living Abroad
11. Biafra of My Dream
12. Breaking Evil Yokes
13. Call to Renew Covenant
14. Command the Morning, Day and Night
15. Community Liberation and Solemn Assembly
16. Comprehensive Deliverance
17. Confront and Conquer Your Enemy
18. Contemporary Politicians' Prayers for Nation Building
19. Crossing the Hurdles
20. Dangerous Decrees to Destroy Your Destroyers (Series)
21. Dealing with Institutional Altars
22. Deliverance by Alpha and Omega
23. Deliverance from Academic Defeats
24. Deliverance from Compromise

An Invitation to Become a Ministry Partner

In response to several calls from readers of my books on how to partner with this ministry, we are grateful to provide our ministry's bank details.

Be assured that our continued prayers for you will be answered according to God's word. And as you remain faithful by sowing seeds of faith, God will never forget your labors of love in Christ.

Send your Seed to:

In Nigeria & Africa

Bank Name: Access Bank

Account Name: Prayer Emancipation Missions

Account Number: 0692638220

In the United States & the rest of the World

Bank Name: Bank of America

Account Name: Roseline C Madueke

Account Number: 483079070578

Routing Number (RTN): 021000322

Visit the donation page on my website to donate online: www.madueke.com/donate.

Made in the USA
Columbia, SC
23 October 2024

44917347R00181